Acclaim for *Women Deacons*

"This is an important and captiv[...] reader step by step on an exciting trail of historical research. The evidence he presents results in an unmistakable and incontrovertible conclusion: women ministered in the early Church as sacramentally ordained deacons. The book is lively in presentation, detailed in academic underpinning and, theologically, extremely relevant to the question of ministry today."

— *René van Eyden, University of Utrecht,
chair of Theology and Feminist Research*

"Wijngaards combines accurate historical inquiry, text analysis, and interpretation of fact with a highly sophisticated theological competence and acute common sense. The text reads like a thriller. Rare indeed are theological books like this."

— *Peter Hünermann, University of Tübingen,
former president of the Catholic Theological
Association of Europe*

"This study clarified some of the basics with regard to the first-millennium diaconate, in which both women and men had an equivalent part. If there is to be an ordained ministry, women ought to be included. John Wijngaards's study can be a jumping-off point for reconnecting ministry in its entirety."

— *Mary Hunt, Women's Alliance for
Theology, Ethics, and Ritual*

"This is an exceptionally engaging and readable book. Wijngaards has also rendered a great service by translating the original sources and presenting them in an easily accessible format. A valuable contribution to academic and church-political discussions."

— *Peter Hofrichter, president of the Institute
of Church History and Patrology*

"The contribution made by John Wijngaards to the ordination debate has been unparalleled by any other English-language writer. His logical analysis is incisive, his academic historical standards are extremely high, and his theology is Catholic through and through, so that the ordination of women emerges as something that is imperative if the Church is to be true to its own nature."

— *Margaret Hebblethwaite, The Tablet*

WOMEN DEACONS IN THE EARLY CHURCH

WOMEN
DEACONS
IN THE
EARLY
CHURCH

*Historical Texts and
Contemporary Debates*

JOHN WIJNGAARDS

A Herder & Herder Book
The Crossroad Publishing Company
New York

The Crossroad Publishing Company
16 Penn Plaza – 481 Eighth Avenue, Suite 1550
New York, NY 10001

First published in the United States in 2006 by The Crossroad Publishing
Company.

First published in 2002 by the Canterbury Press Norwich (a publishing imprint of Hymns Ancient & Modern Limited, a registered
charity) St Mary's Works, St Mary's Plain, Norwich, Norfolk, NR3 3BH.
www.scm-canterburypress.co.uk

Printed in the United States of America

The text of this book is set in 11/15 Sabon.
The display faces are Triplex, Goudy Sans, and Cataneo.

Library of Congress Cataloging-in-Publication Data
Wijngaards, J. N. M.
  Women deacons in the early church : historical texts and contemporary
debates / John Wijngaards.
      p. cm.
  "A Herder & Herder book."
  Includes bibliographical references and index.
  ISBN 0-8245-2393-8 (alk. paper)
  1. Women in Christianity – History – Early church, ca. 30-600.
2. Women clergy – History. 3. Deacons – History. 4. Ordination of
women – Catholic Church. I. Title.
BR195.W6W56 2006
262'.1413082 – dc22
                                                                      2006001119
ISBN-13: 978-0-8245-2393-0

1 2 3 4 5 6 7 8 9 10   12 11 10 09 08 07 06

Illustrations by Jackie Clackson (pp. 16, 71), Alison Conti (p. 4), and Sheila
Gosney (p. 94). The remainder by John Wijngaards.

My special thanks are due to
Jackie Clackson, Roy Barton, Ann Miller,
Barbara Paskins, Mary Simpson, Aloys Wijngaards Sr.,
and Aloys Eduard Wijngaards
for their research, untiring help, and advice.

Contents

Contents

THE ARGUMENT

1

Enigma at Constantinople

IN THE CLASSROOMS and discussion chambers of theologians and church historians alike a battle has raged for over half a century. It has escaped the attention of most Catholics. And yet, the outcome of this clash has serious consequences for the continuing health of the Catholic Church. The debate concerns women deacons during the first millennium. Were they *real* deacons, or were they not? I call it the Olympias enigma. This book is a report on the state of the discussion. Bear with me as I sketch the historical background and outline the views of the two opposing camps.

Imagine the vestibule of Hagia Sophia, the cathedral of Constantinople, at 9:00 a.m. on a normal Sunday morning in the year AD 400.[1] High and low enter through the gate, officials of the imperial court with their retinue, wealthy businessmen and their wives, skilled workers and slaves with their families. They wash their hands in the basin at the center of the vestibule. They have to be pure, for they will take part in the "divine liturgy" and receive holy communion. Now they are received by deacons, the men by male deacons, the women by women deacons.

The senior woman deacon, Olympias, comes forward to greet Anastasia, who is accompanied by her twenty-year-old daughter. Olympias leads them to the women's section in the central nave. Cate-chumens are taken to a special enclosure at the back of the church, for they will be asked to leave the assembly when the sermon and the offertory prayer have been concluded. If Olympias meets a woman she does not know, she welcomes her, but not without diplomatically checking on her credentials: "What is your name? Where are you from? Are you a Christian? Have you been baptized?" At this time

3

Olympias will also hear from relatives about any woman who may be sick and who needs to be visited at home. Perhaps she will make arrangements for the final rites to be administered to the sick person at home, at the end of the liturgy some two hours later. If a priest cannot go, she will take the blessed sacrament herself and perform the anointing of the sick.

The main task of a woman deacon like Olympias was the pastoral care of women. The deacon built up a personal relationship with every woman entrusted to her responsibility. She would instruct her before baptism, often in her own home. During the baptismal ceremony she would undress her and anoint her with the sacred oil of catechumens all over her body. It was she who would immerse her three times in the water of the baptismal font and rub her body dry. She would continue to guide her through various stages of Christian life, provide material help when needed, and nursing when she fell ill. The woman deacon became as intimate a friend as a good neighbor, a social worker, a nurse, a spiritual counselor all rolled in one.

The Church acknowledged this crucial role of women in the ministry. Bishop, male deacon, and woman deacon should work together as the Blessed Trinity, with the woman deacon fulfilling the healing, soothing, steering, and mediating task of the Spirit:

Let the bishop preside over you as one honored with the authority of God, which he is to exercise over the clergy, and by which he is to govern all the people.

But let the deacon minister to him, as Christ does to his Father; and let him serve him unblamably in all things, as Christ
does nothing of himself, but does always those things that please
his Father.

Let also the woman deacon be honored by you in the place
of the Holy Spirit. Let her not do or say anything without the
male deacon; as neither does the Comforter say or do anything
of himself, but gives glory to Christ by waiting for his pleasure.
And as we cannot believe in Christ without the teaching of the
Spirit, so let not any woman address herself to the male deacon
or bishop without the woman deacon. (*Apostolic Constitutions*
II, 26, AD 380)

The Olympias we are talking about in this sketch is St. Olympias.
The patriarch of Constantinople at the time was St. John Chrysostom. The patriarch used to consult her on important ecclesiastical
business. At her request he ordained Elisanthia, Martyria, and Pal-
ladia as "deacons of the holy church."[2] When John was exiled by
Emperor Arcadius in 403, he took leave of her in the baptistery of
the cathedral. He wrote many letters to her from exile, many of which
were addressed: "To my lady, the most reverend and divinely favored
deacon [διακονος] Olympias."[3]

Women like St. Olympias served in the Greek-Byzantine churches
for at least six centuries (200–800). From the ninth century onward
the diaconate of women declined in the East, for a combination of
reasons which I will discuss later. In the West it never really caught
on. As a result, the memory of it was largely lost, except in vague
references. Medieval theologians such as Bonaventure, Richard of
Middleton, Durand of St. Pourçain, John Duns Scotus, and Thomas
Aquinas described it as a mere blessing given to nuns, to autho-
rize them to read out the Gospel in their convents. It was with
some surprise, therefore, that in 1695 Jean Morin of Antwerp, while
researching Greek liturgical manuscripts, stumbled on ancient ordination rites of women deacons. He noted that they were amazingly
similar to the ordination of male deacons. But it was only in the

beginning of the twentieth century that scholars seriously reexamined his discovery.

The liturgist Adolf Kalsbach drew attention to the issue. His colleague Cipriano Vagaggini expressed it to be his considered opinion that the women deacons of the Greek-Byzantine era had received a full sacramental ordination. Roger Gryson, a church historian, concurred, reporting also that women deacons had been treated as clergy in major orders. Meanwhile the Orthodox theologian Evangelos Theodorou had independently arrived at a similar conclusion. Since then an avalanche of scholarship in the East and the West has come to support these findings. But not everyone has fallen into line.

Academic objections

Nicolae Chitescu and Aimé-Georges Martimort strongly contested the emerging reappraisal. They were backed by like-minded theologians. At face value these scholars are making a good case for their position, which I will attempt to summarize here.

Though women deacons *were* ordained in some kind of manner, they say, it was certainly not to receive a major holy order. This can be seen from significant differences in the ordination rite. While male deacons were dedicated to service at the altar, women were barred from any form of sacramental ministry. Male deacons assisted the bishop and priests throughout the eucharist. They read the Gospel, intoned litanies of intercession, prepared the bread and wine for the sacred vessels, and distributed holy communion. None of these actions was permitted to a woman deacon.

Women deacons performed subsidiary functions at baptism, they admit. But these were purely additional to, not part of, the substance of the sacrament itself. For instance, women deacons helped with anointing female catechumens, but it was the bishop or priest himself who imposed the sacramental anointing on the forehead, who immersed the catechumens, and who spoke the Trinitarian formula: "I baptize you in the name of the Father, the Son, and the Holy

Spirit." What women deacons did, any woman could do in the case of need. For this no specific ordination was actually required.

The so-called "diaconate of women," they continue, was in fact no more than a special blessing, as the medieval theologians already taught, a blessing that imparted a spiritual status. It amounted to nothing else than an honorary title, a dignity bestowed on upper-class ladies who had made generous donations to the church or who merited recognition as superiors of religious communities. All these titles fit Olympias to perfection, they say. She hailed from a patrician family, supported the local church financially, and was prioress of a convent of nuns.

And this is not all. If we look at the wider picture, they say, it is obvious that these women did not receive a sacramental order. For all major orders are part of the one sacrament: the eucharistic priest-hood. The same patristic sources that attest to the existence of women deacons emphatically state that women could never be priests. For Jesus Christ chose only men for this ministry and the Church has always honored this tradition. The Church has consistently excluded women from teaching or from any position of authority in spiritual matters. The deeper ground for all this, they contend, lies in God's decision to become incarnate *as a man,* so that only men can adequately represent the incarnate Son of God.

For all these reasons the women deacons of the past were not *real* deacons in today's sense of the term, even though the title "deacon" was applied to them in ancient documents. Their ordination did not confer the real diaconate, even though the rite resembled that of male deacons superficially. The ordaining bishop simply did not have the intention, nor *could* he have had the intention, of imparting to women the full sacramental ordination.

Why does the discussion matter?

Why should we bother about the value of the title "deacon" given to women like Olympias and other women in the past? It seems the kind of thing academics quibble about, like whether a particular prehistoric heel bone belonged to an *Iguanodon,* a *Triceratops,* or a *Struthiomimus.* Of historical interest sure, but hardly a conundrum that will keep us awake at night. However, the comparison fails.

The real issue at stake behind this seemingly obtuse jousting by university professors is a question that rocks the Catholic Church of our time: "Can women be ordained *priests?*" In spite of the quite legitimate distinction between diaconate and priesthood as separate ministries, the women deacons of the past are inextricably linked with a wider inquiry about holy orders themselves. For if the diaconate of women was a true diaconate, if it was one valid expression of the sacrament of *holy orders,* then women did in fact receive holy orders and the priesthood too is open to them.

I am aware that some theologians disagree with me. They contend that it would be perfectly possible for the Catholic Church to separate the two ministries in such a way that women could be given the sacrament of the diaconate, even though the priesthood was withheld from them. This is, for instance, the opinion of the Orthodox bishop Kallistos Ware[4] and the Catholic theologian Phyllis Zagano.[5] I believe that they are mistaken for two important reasons: a historical one and a church-political one. The admission to the diaconate and the priesthood will not so easily be separated in the Catholic Church.

On July 15, 1563, the Council of Trent declared that "in the Catholic Church there exists a hierarchy by divine ordination instituted, consisting of bishops, priests, and deacons." The implication is that the Council considered all three major orders, including the diaconate, as fully sacramental, without fully resolving their inner connection.[6] On account of this and of the traditional reasons for which women were barred from ordination, Catholic scholars generally see the question of women's admission to the diaconate as linked to their admission to the priestly ministry.

This is the opinion of the liturgist Hans Jorissen: "The possibility of women receiving the sacramental diaconate stands or falls with the possibility of women receiving the priesthood."[7] His view is shared by the theologian Dirk Ansorge: "If women are ordained deacons, the unity of the sacrament of holy orders will demand their access to the sacramental priesthood."[8] The canon lawyer Charles Wilson expressed it in this way:

> If the Church does admit women to diaconal ordination, it seems to me that this action would give rise to the formidable challenge of performing the difficult mental gymnastics involved in asserting that women can validly be admitted to one grade of orders while at the same time reaffirming the definitive teaching of the Church that they cannot be admitted to the others.[9]

The scope of this book

It will now be clear why I am writing this book. Once the sacramentality of women's diaconate in the past is established, the question regarding women's ordination to the priesthood will have been resolved in principle. An old Church adage comes into play here: *Ex facto sequitur posse,* which means, from the fact that the Church *has* done something it follows that she *can* do it. If the Church did ordain women in the past, she can do so now.

It is my considered opinion that the exclusion of women from the priestly ministry is due to complex social and cultural prejudices against women in previous centuries, prejudices that disguised themselves under spurious theological argumentation. I have labeled this a cuckoo's-egg tradition.[10] Could the *Titanic* of ecclesiastical bias against women in holy orders be heading for its shipwreck on the iceberg of a simple historical fact, the undeniable precedent of ordained women deacons?

Leaving the link with *priestly* ordination aside for the moment, I want to settle once and for all the historicity of this sacramental ordination of women deacons. This explains the structure of the book. The first part moves from presentation (chapters 1–5) and debate (chapters 6–12) to the final assessment (chapters 13–15). The second part, the Texts, merits a special word of introduction.

When I was a teenager — an incredible fifty years ago! — a new brand of detective story captured people's imagination. It came as a complete set. The cardboard cover that contained the book also held the "clues" available to the police: a fold-out plan of the house where the murder had been committed, photographs of the victim *in situ,* signed statements of the chief suspects, a copy of a handwritten will, incriminating rail tickets, and so on. It enabled the reader to check the evidence while digesting the story. This book follows a similar strategy. The chapters take you step by step through the debate in what is hopefully a readable manner. At the same time the historical records are offered for inspection in the Texts section.

The Vatican's International Theological Commission has re-affirmed that the diaconate belongs to the sacrament of orders. It also came to the — somewhat fuzzy — conclusion that the women's diaconate in the early Church was not "simply equivalent" with the male diaconate — whatever that means. As a result, the Congregation for the Doctrine of the Faith is expected to pronounce its definitive "NO" to women deacons. "The Church does not have the authority to ordain women to be deacons. End of discussion!" Should that happen, this book will prove them wrong. The Church did impart to women a full, equivalent, sacramental diaconate, and so it *does have* the power to ordain women.

This book has one other unique feature. It is closely linked to information that can be found on the Internet at *www.womenpriests.org.* As a Catholic Internet library on women's ordination, this Web site stores many more documents than can be printed even in ten volumes. The information contained in this book will be enriched, and constantly updated, by further material posted on the Internet. For a survey on all current documentation regarding the ancient women deacons, go straight to *www.womenpriests.org/deacons/default.asp.*

2

The evidence for women deacons

IF WE COULD HAVE visited a Christian community during the first century of the Church's existence, we would have met three kinds of ministers: "overseers" (*episcopoi*), "elders" (*presbyteroi*), and "servants" (*diakonoi*). We might also have observed that these ministers were dedicated by the community to their task through prayer and the imposition of hands. The apostles prayed and laid their hands on the newly selected deacons (Acts 6:6). Paul and Barnabas "laid their hands on elders" in Lystra and Iconium, "dedicating them with prayer to the Lord" (Acts 14:23).[1] Later Paul addressed the assembled *elders* of the communities of Asia Minor when he passed through Miletus. He urged them to care for their flock "over whom the Holy Spirit has made you *episcopoi*" (Acts 20:28). By the time St. Ignatius, bishop of Antioch, died for his faith (AD 110), the three ministries of bishop, presbyter, and deacon were widely established.

But it would be a mistake to imagine that these three functions had the same contents that they have for us today. In the course of the centuries so much changed, with variations between different countries as well, that it is difficult even to summarize the enormous shifts that took place. All I can do is to sketch some of the major developments.

The ministry that is most clearly recognizable in today's terms would have been that of the bishop. He had full pastoral charge of the local community and presided over its eucharist. In many respects he did what a parish priest does today. Only gradually did bishops acquire authority over wider areas, which brought with it the coordinating and supervising roles now enjoyed by diocesan bishops.

11

When we speak of a priest today, we are inclined to think of him as a person who receives spiritual power that enables him to offer the sacrifice of Mass and administer the sacraments. For many Catholics a "priest" is what is technically known as a *sacerdos,* a sacrificial priest, using a term derived from the Temple in Jerusalem and Roman pagan practice. But this is not what "elder," presbyter, stood for in the early Church. During the first two centuries there existed no *sacerdos,* except for Christ.[2] The whole people of God was sacerdotal. From the third century onward the bishop is at times called the *sacerdos* of his community, but this is not applied to the elders. Originally these were not even allowed to preside over a eucharist. Only gradually, in small places where there was no bishop, elders began to preside at the eucharist. They had become *second-rank bishops.*[3] But only the Middle Ages shaped the theology of the individual sacred priestly "character" that would dominate Church thinking until Vatican II.

The ministry of deacons too underwent many changes. The Acts of the Apostles report that seven men were ordained deacon to care for the poor. Soon afterward we hear of the deacon Stephen preaching and performing miracles. And the deacon Philip preached and baptized in Samaria (Acts 6:1–6; 6:7–7:60; 8:4–40). Later we find deacons entrusted with pastoral work, baptism, and service at solemn liturgies. They were much closer to the bishop than the presbyters, and often much more influential. During St. John Chrysostom's time, the management of all church property, as well as the care of the poor, the sick, and widows, the upkeep of churches and cemeteries — in a word the entire government of the temporal affairs of the Church — lay in the hands of the deacons. Chrysostom enumerates as sources of church income: "fields, houses, rents from dwellings, vehicles, packhorses, mules, and much more of that kind of thing." At least this was the case in Antioch and Constantinople.[4]

The point I am trying to make is that the ministries varied greatly in contents, status, and function from place to place and from one era to the next. It would be a mistake to generalize.[5] And the same shifting patterns can be observed regarding women's ministries.

Women in the diaconate

Women deacons have not been a constant or universal phenomenon in the history of the Church. They served communities in the eastern half of the Christian world during the first millennium. Then they slowly disappeared from the scene. And we should remind ourselves from the start that our information about the first ten centuries of the Church is incomplete. Yes, the writings of the Fathers tell their story, and so do ancient documents and archeological sites, and yet these reveal only glimpses of what must have been a very colorful and varied tale. Antioch in Syria, for instance, one of the principal centers of Christian life, lost its collection of patristic writings in 637 during the Islamic invasion. The same fate befell Alexandria in 642. Constantinople's libraries were sacked by the Crusaders in 1207 and by the Ottoman army in 1453. Moreover, the fragmentary sources preserved elsewhere do not contain full or systematic descriptions of church life. Much is taken for granted, since people at the time would not normally record things familiar to their contemporaries. A common practice is often mentioned only in passing. Add to this that most writing was done on flimsy papyrus, which is a perishable material anyway.

What do we know, in spite of this? St. Paul's letters mention a number of Christian women in the ministry by name:

- "Greet Prisca and Aquila my fellow workers in Christ Jesus" ... "Greet Mary who has worked so much among you." In the same way "Tryphaena, Tryphosa, and Persis labor in the Lord" ... "Junia ... outstanding among the Apostles" (Romans 16:3–15). Paul certainly refers here to apostolic tasks (Romans 16:1–16).[6] John Chrysostom commented, "Andronicus and Junia ... who are outstanding among the apostles! To be an apostle is something great. But to be outstanding among the apostles — just think what a wonderful song of praise that is! They were outstanding on the basis of their works and virtuous actions. Indeed, how great the wisdom of this woman must have been that she was even deemed worthy of the title of apostle!"[7]

- "Euodia and Syntyche, who have struggled together with me in the Gospel with Clement and the rest of my fellow-workers" (Philippians 4:2–3). "In the Gospel" surely implies participation in the work of evangelism (Philippians 4:2).[8]

- "Phoebe, our sister, who is a servant [διακονος] of the Church at Cenchreae. She has often been a helper both to myself and to many others" (Romans 16:1).

The word *diakonos* (masculine noun!) applied to Phoebe, may well carry the sense of the ministerial function which already existed in Paul's time, however much the various ministries were still in development. In the letter to the Philippians Paul sends greetings to "the bishops and deacons" (Philippians 1:1). And since we know that deacons were ordained — "the apostles prayed and laid their hands on them" — we have no reason to exclude the possibility that Phoebe too was ordained to the diaconate (cf. Acts 6:6).[9]

This early diaconate of women is further testified to in a classical passage in 1 Timothy dated to about AD 100: "Deacons must be men of grave behavior; they must be examined and if found blameless may afterward serve as deacons. The women must be of grave behavior, not slanderers, temperate, in every respect faithful. Deacons must be married only once" (1 Timothy 3:8–12). The whole passage is about those serving in the diaconate, both men and women. Cardinal Daniélou, who defended the ordained status of the women's diaconate, writes as follows: "The word 'deacon' is here used in its technical sense. It also seems clear that by 'the women' in question, who are clearly distinguished from the wives of the deacons while the description of them is parallel to that of the deacons, we must understand *women deacons*. It indicates a ministry which formed part of the ordained ministry itself."[10] Many scholars agree: "These women in the ministry are mentioned in the same breath as their male colleagues and seem to be treated as fully equal."[11]

The diaconate of women is also mentioned in other early sources. Pliny, procurator of Asia Minor, reports in a letter to the emperor that he has arrested a number of Christians, among them their leaders. "All the more it seemed necessary to me to find out the truth, even by applying torture, from these two slave women, who were called 'ministrae' [διακονοι?]" (AD 111).[12]

St. Clement of Alexandria (150–215) testifies to women deacons, ascribing tasks to them that would still be entrusted to ordained women deacons centuries later:

> The apostles, giving themselves without respite to the work of evangelism as befitted their ministry, took with them women, not as wives but as sisters, so that they might serve as their co-ministers [συνδιακονους], serving women living at home: by their agency the teaching of the Lord reached the women's quarters without arousing suspicion. We are also aware of all the things Paul prescribed on the subject of women deacons in one of the two letters to Timothy.[13]

Origen (c. 185–254), a Christian scholar in the Alexandrian community, comments on women's diaconate as a valuable institution:

> The text [1 Timothy 3:11] teaches with the authority of the Apostle that even women are established as deacons in the Church. This was the function that was exercised in the community of Cenchreae by Phoebe.... This pious Phoebe, while offering help and service to all, deserved to assist and serve the Apostle himself. And thus this text teaches at the same time two things: that there are, as I have said, women deacons in the Church, and that women, who have given assistance to so many people and who by their good works deserve to be praised by the Apostle, ought to be accepted in the diaconate.[14]

It is indisputable, therefore, that women deacons existed during those early centuries, together with other groups of women who seem to have had distinct tasks in the Christian communities.

Ministries for and by women

In the second and third centuries women continued to be involved in the apostolate. This certainly included looking after the physical and material welfare of women, instructing catechumens, welcoming strangers, placing orphaned children with foster parents, visiting the sick, mediating in quarrels, advising bishops and priests on the needs of their parishioners. The organization of these ministries for women seems to have varied from place to place.

There were the *prophetesses*. Philip the Evangelist had four daughters who "prophesied" (Acts 21:9). Paul had written, "Every man who prays or who prophesies with his head covered dishonors his head. Every woman who prays or prophesies with her head unveiled dishonors her head" (1 Corinthians 11:4–5).[15] He put prophesying by a woman on the same plane as prophesying by a man.

The *widows* too had distinct tasks: "They must teach what is good and train the young women to love their husbands and children" (Titus 2:3–4). They soon became an organized group: "Before she can be inscribed on the roll, a widow must be sixty years old at least, once married, one who has practiced hospitality, washed the feet of the saints, and been given to all good works" (1 Timothy 5:3–10). The interesting point is the enrolment on a register and the conditions it implies, for this makes it plain that we are concerned here not with all the widows, but with some of their number who constitute a special category within the community. Ignatius of Antioch greets "the virgins and the order of widows."[16] The widows became quite prominent as we can see from other contemporary writings.

The relationship between widows and *women deacons* is often blurred in early records. The *Apostolic Tradition* of St. Hippolytus of Rome (AD 220) states that widows are not ordained, but deacons are. It does not indicate whether these deacons included women. It is only in the third century that some local churches clarified the position of women deacons with more precision, possibly because of problems with the overlapping functions of the widows. In the *Didascalia* (third century) and the *Apostolic Constitutions* (fourth century) the distinct roles of "widow" and "woman deacon" are beginning to be spelled out.

Elaborate ceremonies had grown around the Christian sacraments, especially baptism and the anointing of the sick. These required the help of dedicated women, specifically *ordained* for such tasks. Women deacons were the obvious choice. The full recognition of Christianity by Emperor Constantine resulted in more adult baptisms, and this in turn boosted the need of more ordained deacons. Some historians believe that the ordination of women to the full diaconate dates from this period.[17] Whether this is true, or whether the Church simply enhanced a practice already started in apostolic times, from now on a complete sacramental ordination became the norm for the Byzantine part of the Church.

For this book I have decided to leave the first two centuries out of our discussion. For we do not possess accurate information about the *sacramental status* of women deacons during those two centuries. We simply lack the evidence. We have information starting from 250 and then impressive data flowing in from 400. In the chapters that follow we shall therefore focus on the women deacons in the golden period of the Greek-Byzantine empire. This roughly spans seven centuries: from 300 to 1000, and covers Asia Minor, Greece, Cyprus, Syria, and the Greek-speaking colonies of southern Italy. Remember that these regions still formed part of the universal "Catholic Church" at the time. The split between East and West didn't occur until 1054!

What are our sources about women deacons from AD 200?

In chapter 11, I will present the evidence from archaeology, the lives of saints, and early correspondence. As to the written records, I have translated anew and printed out the most important ones in the Texts section, and I will characterize them briefly here.

The *Didascalia apostolorum* (250), a pastoral handbook, urges bishops to ordain men and women deacons. It outlines their respective tasks. It goes into tantalizing detail. Though originally the private work of a Greek author, it was translated into Syriac, Arabic, and Latin, and attained some standing in the Church.

The Council of Nicea I (325) witnessed to the existence of women deacons. It declares that women deacons are not ordained, but this assessment seems to refer to women deacons among the followers of Paul of Samosata.

The Greek Fathers of the third, fourth, and fifth centuries mention women deacons. Among them are Clement of Alexandria, Epiphanius, Basil of Caesarea, John Chrysostom, Theodore of Mopsuestia, and Theodoret of Cyrrhus.

The *Apostolic Constitutions* (380), another collection of pastoral directives, repeated the instructions on women deacons already found in the *Didascalia* and proposed some alterations. It also preserved the oldest known ordination rite for women deacons.

The Council of Chalcedon (451) discussed the diaconate of women, prescribing for it the minimum age of forty years as a condition for ordination. This was repeated by the Council of Trullo (692). Since these were general councils of the whole Church, their ruling shows that the ordination of women deacons was, in principle, a practice sanctioned for the universal Church — even if the practice actually did not get much of a foothold in the West. The official status of the women's diaconate is also confirmed by detailed legislation under Emperor Justinian I of Constantinople (527–65), which attributed an equal legal position to men and women deacons.

And, of course, we have the ancient ordination rite preserved in Byzantine liturgical books. We will see more about this in the next chapter.

3

The manuscripts
that preserved the rite

THE OLDEST ORDINATION RITE for women deacons comes from the *Apostolic Constitutions* (AD 380). The full text can be read in Texts, p. 158. Though the rite is brief, most commentators believe it has all the hallmarks of a full sacramental ordination.[1] It is also substantially identical to the ordination of a male deacon. However, the matter is even clearer in the standard ordination rite which can be traced back to the fifth century and which has been preserved for us in many documents.

Until the invention of printing in 1450, important texts were copied from one generation to the next by hand. "Manuscript" means "handwritten document." At the time of Christ the most frequently used material to write on was *papyrus*, sheets made of a pulp of reeds. Papyrus was the forerunner of our present-day paper. But writing on papyrus required patience and ingenuity because of its unequal texture. And it did not last. In the second century BC, traders in the Greek city of Pergamum invented a new material made from the skins of sheep, goats, or calves. It became known as *parchment*. By carefully processing the skins, through cleaning, stretching, and scraping, thin sheets of fine leather were produced both sides of which could be written on. When a number of these sheets were bound together, they formed a book. The technical name for this is *codex*.

The ordination rites of women deacons for the period we are interested in have been preserved in the following ten precious manuscripts. We list them here with their library catalogue numbers. The codices in question are books that list and describe the prayers and rubrics needed by a bishop for various occasions. In the Latin tradition we call such a book a *rituale*; in the Greek tradition it is known as an *euchologion*:

- the Codex Barberini — Vatican Library gr. 336 (AD 780)[2]
- the Bessarion Codex — Grottaferrata Γβ 1 (ninth/tenth century)[3]
- the Sinai Codex — gr. 956 (tenth century)[4]
- the Paris Codex — Coislinus gr. 213 (AD 1027)[5]
- the Messina Codex — Oxford, Bodleian auct. E.5.13 (AD 1130)[6]
- Codex Vaticanus gr. 1872 (twelfth century)[7]
- Codex Vaticanus gr. 1970 (twelfth century)[8]
- the Athens Codex — National Library of Greece ms. 662 (twelfth–fourteenth centuries)[9]
- the Cairo Codex — library of the Patriarchate of Alexandria gr. 104 (fourteenth century)[10]
- the Mount Athos Codex — St. Xenophon monastery gr. 163 (fourteenth century)[11]

As said, the listed codices are *euchologia*, i.e., liturgical books which present the eucharistic prayers, the presidential prayers of the liturgy of the hours, the rites of the sacraments, and a large collection of blessings and prayers for various situations and necessities. They also contain — and this is most important for us — the rites of ordaining a bishop, a priest, a male deacon, a woman deacon, and installing subdeacons, lectors, acolytes, and so on. But how can we determine their age? And how are we sure that the ordination rites described reflect a Church practice that goes back to at least 550? Let us study the evidence in a sample case.

Barberini gr. 336

At present this codex is kept in the Vatican Library. We know it arrived there in 1902, when Pope Leo XIII acquired a valuable collection of ancient manuscripts that had belonged to Cardinal Francis

Barberini. This explains its name: Greek manuscript no. 336 in the Barberini collection.

Now Francesco Barberini (1597–1679) was a colorful character who belonged to a powerful family. He had been created a cardinal by his uncle Pope Urban VIII in October 1623. The Barberinis sponsored Renaissance sculptors and architects, collected art treasures, and built magnificent churches and palaces. Francesco's brother, Antonio the Younger, who also had been made a cardinal, started the Barberini collection of ancient books, a collection which after Antonio's death became the property of Francesco. For a while the Barberini fortune was eclipsed due to a defeat of their armies by the Farnese family and the death of Urban VIII. Francesco spent nine years in exile with Cardinal Mazarin in Paris, but in 1653 he was allowed to return to Rome, where he lived another twenty-five years in the luxury of the Barberini Palace.

The Barberinis originally hailed from Florence, and they were friendly with the Florentine senator Carlo Strozzi (1587–1670). It is through Strozzi that they acquired the collection of books found in the library of the Dominican Convent of St. Mark. Our codex had been part of that collection for some centuries. We know this from notes written on the codex by monastic librarians. On the back of the outside cover, we find an annotation which must, perhaps, be attributed to the hand of Zenobi Acciaiuoli (1461–1519), librarian in the Convent of St. Mark until 1513: "Prayers of the Mass and of the whole office according to St. Basil. Convent of St. Mark in Florence of the Order of the Brothers Preachers belonging to the in-heritance of Nicolai de Nicholis." Also we find the numbering and location which the codex had received: "33. on the first shelf towards the East." Also we find on *folium* 1 (sheet 1): "Prayers of the Mass according to St. Basil and prayers of the whole office and a way of containing heretics"; and on *folium* 17, the last annotation: "The Office of the Greeks."

The reading room of the Florentine Convent of St. Mark owed its existence to Cosimo de Medici (1389–1464), who established it as one of the first public libraries of modern times. And remember that the librarian had noted, "belonging to the inheritance of Nicolai de Nicholis." This gives us a clue to its earlier ownership. It had been bequeathed to the library in 1441 by the humanist and book lover Nicholas Nicoli (1363–1437), who had in his lifetime collected a magnificent collection of codices. Where did Nicholas obtain the codex from?

The codex had been used for centuries as episcopal *euchologion* by a succession of Greek-Byzantine bishops in Italy.[12] For how long? We can only speculate here, but it seems likely that the *euchologion* had been withdrawn from liturgical use in the tenth or eleventh century. The reason was the fact that the ancient uncial characters — about which more later — could no longer be easily read in those days. This is clear from some marginal notes in Greek cursive script dating to that time. We may presume that some time in the eleventh century it moved from a cathedral sacristy to a monastic library or to the personal bookshelf of an ecclesiastic. It must have been sold to a merchant during the time when Renaissance collectors were looking for antique books.

Where did the copyist who wrote out the copy actually perform his work? Internal evidence shows links both to Constantinople and to Greek-speaking communities in Italy. Some scholars think the copy was written in Constantinople and then almost immediately after completion transported to Italy. Others believe it was written in Italy itself, but from a copy that had come from Constantinople. Can we fix the date of the copying?

When was the codex written?

The book can be dated, first of all, by its physical appearance. The condition of the parchment, the cover, and the binding all have their tale to tell. Jean Morin, who examined the codex in the Barberini library in 1655, wrote: "This is a most beautiful codex, venerable in antiquity and majesty!"[13]

Then we can study the form of writing. See the illustration on the following page. It contains the beginning of the ordination of male deacons, the rubrics being slightly smaller than the prayer.[14] It is *folium* 336, which shows the start of the ordination rite. In early Greek manuscripts, letters were written in capitals with no separation between the words. This is known as *majuscule* script (see also Illustration II on p. 139). Originally the capital letters were square, but gradually they became more rounded, resulting in *curved uncial* script. This script was replaced in everyday usage by so-called *minuscule* script — lowercase letters with spaces between the words — in the eighth and ninth centuries (see Illustrations III and IV, pp. 140 and 141).

Describing Barberini gr. 336, Morin wrote, "This beautiful codex has been written in capitals and uncials, not square ones of time, developed from the square form. To anyone who is used to dealing with ancient Greek codices, this copy cannot be younger than 800 years, perhaps even exceeding that age by many years."[15] Since Morin saw the codex in 1655, he dated it to before 850.

In our own days, scholars see confirmation of its antiquity in evidence from texts that form part of the *euchologion*. In the Anaphora (eucharistic prayer) of Chrysostom we read this intercession: "for the most trustworthy kings, and for the queen beloved by Christ" (§37.4). The kings in question could perhaps be identified with Constantine VI of the Syriac Dynasty (780–97) and Mary, whom he married in 788, or his second wife, Theodota, whom he married in 795; the queen could not have been anyone other than Irene, the wife of Leo IV (775–80). If so, the codex must have been copied before 788 or 797.

Or again, consider the following. One of the prayers of the kind read "from the ambo," the second in the collection copied toward the end of the codex (§274.1), is attributed to "the Patriarch Germanus," who can be identified with Germanus I of Constantinople (715–30), who died in 733. The copy could therefore not have been written before 715. Another prayer, this time in Latin and of Nordic tradition, copied on the back of *folium* 279, gives another clue. The prayer, though in Latin, was inserted by a Greek hand and destined for the blessing of milk and honey. Because of its specific context and content, it can be dated to around 800, with an uncertainty margin of twenty years.

For all such reasons experts date the codex to around 780.[16] But the rites contained in the codex are much earlier.

Dating the ordination rite itself

The ten codices I have listed above all contain the ordinations normally performed by Byzantine bishops, including the ordination of women deacons. Even a cursory examination of the various versions in these codices shows that they are remarkably uniform. It is clear that we are dealing with an ancient tradition. The stress is not on new inventions, but on faithfully preserving what was done before. Both rubrics and texts were scrupulously copied to ensure that the ordaining bishop would be able to follow the practice of the forefathers and say the ordination prayers laid down long ago. To make study of the text easier, I have printed the text from eight of the codices in the Texts section, pp. 175–188. Let us see this in an example.

The first invocation of the Holy Spirit over the woman candidate begins with these lines:

> Holy and Omnipotent Lord, through the birth of your Only Son our God from a Virgin according to the flesh, you have sanctified the female sex. You grant not only to men, but also to women the grace and coming of the Holy Spirit. Please, Lord, look on this your maidservant and dedicate her to the task of your diaconate, and pour out into her the rich and abundant giving of your Holy Spirit. (Barberini gr. 336; Byzantine communities in Italy, 780)

> Holy and Omnipotent Lord, through the birth of your Only Son our God from a Virgin according to the flesh, you have sanctified the female sex. You grant not only to men, but also to women the grace and coming (from above) of the Holy Spirit. Please, Lord, look on this your maidservant and dedicate her to the task of your diaconate, and pour out into her the rich and abundant giving of your Holy Spirit. (Bessarion Codex; copied in Constantinople around 1020. George Varus, a priest from Crete, had given it to Cardinal Julian of St. Sabina during the Council of Florence [1438–45].)

> Holy and Omnipotent Lord, through the birth of your Only Son our God from a Virgin according to the flesh, you have sanctified the female sex. You grant not only to men, but also to women the grace and coming of the Holy Spirit. Please, Lord, look on this your maidservant and dedicate her to the task of your diaconate, and pour out into her the rich and abundant giving of your Holy Spirit. (Codex Coislinus gr. 213; "euchologion of the Great Church in Constantinople," AD 1027).[17]

In spite of a three hundred years' difference in time span between the copying, all three manuscripts carry virtually an identical text. This applies especially to the prayer parts of the rite. The invocations and prayers were considered the most sacred and most unalterable element in the rite.

Even in the rubrics there are only minor variations. These adaptations show that the rite was not a dead text. Compare how the beginning of the ordination is described in various codices:

> After the sacred offertory, the doors [of the sanctuary] are opened and, before the deacon starts the litany "All Saints," the woman who is to be ordained deacon is brought before the bishop. (Barberini gr. 336; AD 780)

> After the sacred offertory, the doors [of the sanctuary] are opened and, before the deacon starts the litany "All Saints," the woman who is to ordained deacon is brought up. (Grottaferrata Γβ 1; AD 1020)

> [The woman to be ordained deacon] must have lived as a chaste virgin and now be single, of good bearing, without exaggerated hairdo, and eminent in character to such an extent that she can truly stand up also to men and earn their respect. For such a woman candidate all [ritual] is performed that is also performed for male deacons, with only a few differences. For she is led to the sacred altar, her head covered by her [woman's] veil, with the two tips of it in front [over her shoulders]. (Coislin gr. 213; AD 1027)

> After the sacred offertory, the woman who is to be ordained deacon is brought before the archbishop. (Vaticanus gr. 1872, twelfth century)

The minor changes in the text, apart from demonstrating that the rite was actually performed in a variety of contexts, also help us to reconstruct the original form of the rite. The ten codices may be compared to racehorses whose genetic code allows us to trace a common ancestor.

Though copies of codices were made in many locations — Constantinople, Cyprus, Athens, Alexandria, Italy, and so on — we can build a family tree which shows the relationship between the text in various manuscripts. The texts in Barberini gr. 336, Xenophon gr. 163, and Bodleian E.5.13 are almost identical. They were all copied from a "master" in what I call "family A." The texts in the Grottaferrata Γβ 1 codex, Sinai gr. 956, and Vatican gr. 1872 show matching variations. To mention but one: the litany by the deacon is abbreviated. This could go back to "family B." Codex Coislin gr. 213 and Cairo gr. 104 have the same initial paragraph with the condition that the candidate should be someone "who must have lived as a chaste virgin and who is, according to present legislation, single, of good bearing, without exaggerated hairdo, and eminent in character to such an extent that she can truly stand up also to men and earn their respect. For such a woman candidate all is performed that is also performed for male deacons, with only a few differences." The text in these two codices derives from a source that I call "family C."

A look at the diagram on page 28 puts these various codices and their relationships within a framework of time. It shows that already in the sixth and seventh centuries various models of the ordination text existed which go back to an even more ancient parent model. All the later manuscripts we have reflect that early model. I have not been able to complete a thorough research on this, for the matter is extremely complex. We know that various Byzantine codices were modeled on a number of *typicons,* i.e., models popular with copyists. Among them we find the typicon of the patriarchal liturgy of the Hagia Sophia in Constantinople and the typicon of the convent of women religious of the Most Sacred Favored Mother of God in Constantinople. Even if copyists used one particular typicon for the major part of their codex, they added prayers from other typicons as well.

We know that the ordination of women declined in the Greek-Byzantine churches from the eleventh century onward, for reasons we will discuss later. The fact that the rite was still faithfully copied in later manuscripts proves its antiquity, and the unwillingness of church authorities to give up sections of the *euchologion* that had

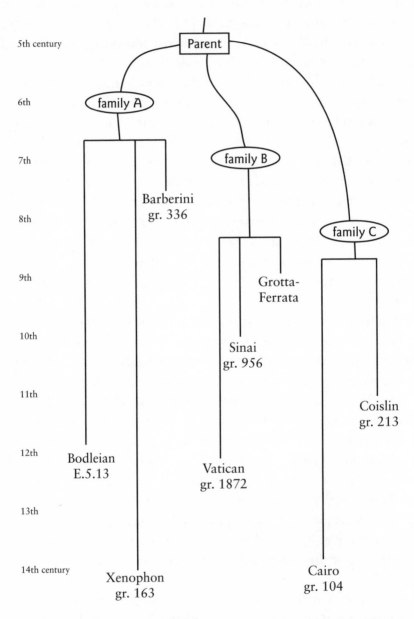

5th century

6th

7th

8th

9th

10th

11th

12th

13th

14th century

Parent

family A

family B

family C

Barberini
gr. 336

Grotta-
Ferrata

Sinai
gr. 956

Coislin
gr. 213

Bodleian
E.5.13

Vatican
gr. 1872

Xenophon
gr. 163

Cairo
gr. 104

Sketch of a possible family tree of the manuscripts. The relationships are based
on an analysis of the variations in the rubrics of the ordination of women
deacons. See the Texts section.

been handed on, even if those sections were no longer immediately relevant.

The rite for the ordination of women deacons described in the standard Byzantine *euchologion*, as exemplified in the ten codices listed above, represents a well-established practice that dates from around 500 and that covered all the countries where the Byzantine liturgy was celebrated.

4

The rite of ordaining a woman deacon

FROM APOSTOLIC TIMES, deacons have been enrolled into their ministry by ordination. When the seven first deacons had been selected in AD 34 or 35, "the apostles prayed and laid their hands on them" (Acts 6:6). This practice has continued throughout the centuries until our own day. Neither can there be any doubt about the ordination to the diaconate being part of the Church's sacramental order, even if we admit huge changes in the diaconate ministry from one period to the next. On the terms of the Council of Trent, the diaconate is a true sacrament and forms part of what we now call "holy orders." And the Second Vatican Council teaches:

> Hands are imposed upon deacons, not unto the priesthood but unto a ministry of service. For strengthened by the grace of the sacrament, in communion with the bishop and his college of priests, they serve the people of God in the ministry of the liturgy, of the word, and of charity.[1]

Women deacons were ordained in the early Catholic Byzantine Church by means of the same ordination rite as male deacons. This fact is crucial. The diaconate ministry was entrusted both to the man and to the woman through identical sacramental signs. As we discussed in the previous chapter, the standard rite used can be found in the official Byzantine *euchologion,* i.e., a ritual book containing detailed instructions on the ceremonies and prayers to be used at the ordination of bishops, priests, deacons, subdeacons, readers, acolytes, and doorkeepers.

In this chapter we will follow the ordination rite for women deacons as handed on in the Grottaferrata Γβ 1, also known as the

Bessarion codex or the *patriarchal euchologion*. Allow me to introduce this manuscript a little more in detail. It owes its name to the fact that it was copied in Constantinople itself around 1020, following the rites "used by the patriarch." It served a bishop in Cyprus. Then, during the Council of Florence (1438–45), a priest from Crete called George Varus gave it to Cardinal Julian of St. Sabina in Rome. The cardinal passed it on to the Catholic Byzantine monastery of St. Nilus in Grottaferrata.

To present the ordination within its proper setting, I will place it within the full Byzantine eucharistic liturgy.

The opening part of the eucharist

The liturgy starts with the solemn entrance. The bishop and his retinue process through the nave of the church to the iconostasis, the sacred screen that divides the body of the church, where the faithful stand, from the sanctuary which surrounds the altar. This screen is about six feet high. It owes its name to the icons of Christ, Mary, and the Apostles that adorn its front. When the bishop, priests, and deacons have entered the sanctuary, the "holy doors" of the iconostasis are closed. Unseen by the faithful, the bishop kisses the altar and then takes his seat in the apse. The priests and deacons vest. The deacon and principal priest bring the gifts from a side table, the *prothesis,* to the altar and prepare the sacred vessels for the eucharist. This is a long ceremony. The host is put on the paten, the *diskos,* with elaborate ritual, and the wine is poured into the chalice, also with elaborate ritual and many prayers. Both the paten and the chalice are covered with veils. The bishop is then invited to come and finish the blessing of the gifts.

Then the deacon says, "For the offering of the honorable gifts, let us pray to the Lord." The bishop takes the censer and says the prayer of offering:

O God, our God, who didst send forth the heavenly Bread, the food of the whole world, our Lord and God Jesus Christ, Savior,

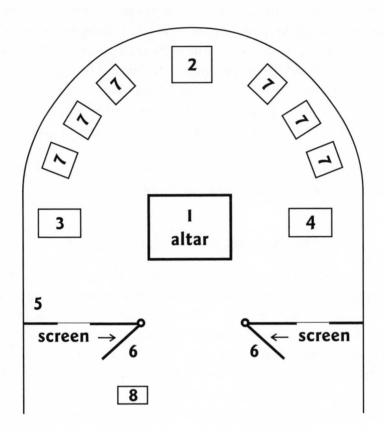

1. The altar, also called the "holy table," the "sacred throne."
2. The bishop's chair.
3. The *deacon's table,* which holds the liturgical vestments of priests and deacons, the books and the sacred vessels.
4. The *prothesis,* the credence table for the gifts: bread, wine, and water.
5. The *iconostasis,* or sacred screen, that separates the sanctuary from the nave.
6. The holy doors in the sacred screen.
7. Chairs for priests.
8. The ambo, or lectern, from which the readings are read.

DIAGRAM OF THE SANCTUARY

Redeemer, and Benefactor, blessing and sanctifying us, do thou thyself bless this offering and receive it upon thy most heavenly altar....

The deacon then incenses the gifts on the altar. Walking around the altar he incenses it on all sides; then he incenses the whole sanctuary and walking into the nave incenses the people and the images on the iconostasis.

The lector now reads from the ambo outside the screen. The first reading is usually taken from the Old Testament and the second from the letters of the Apostles. The Gospel book is then blessed, carried by the deacon in a small procession through the holy doors of the screen to the ambo where he reads or sings the Gospel text. The deacon returns the Gospel book, and the holy doors are closed again.

The sermon follows, usually preached by the bishop himself. After this there are prayers for the catechumens, who are then dismissed from the church. The holy doors are opened, and while the deacon completes a new round of incensing, the bishop says this silent prayer about the sanctity required by the ministers of the holy mysteries:

None is worthy among those that are bound with carnal desires and pleasures to approach or draw nigh or to minister to thee, O King of glory, for to serve thee is a great and fearful thing even unto the heavenly Powers. Nevertheless, through thine ineffable and immeasurable love of human beings, without change or alteration, thou didst become human and didst take the name of our High Priest, and deliver unto us the priestly rite of this liturgical and bloodless sacrifice, for thou art Master of all. Thou alone, O Lord our God, art Master over those in heaven and on earth, who on the throne of the Cherubim art borne, who art Lord of the Seraphim and King of Israel, who alone art holy and restest in the Saints....

This is the moment within the eucharistic service when the ordination to the diaconate takes place.

Public election of the candidate

From here on we will cite the rubrics and prayers as found in
the Bessarion Codex (Grottaferrata Γβ 1). The original text will be
presented in bold sans serif type:

> **After the sacred offertory, the doors [of the sanctuary] are**
> **opened and, before the deacon starts the litany "All Saints,"**
> **the woman who is to be ordained deacon is brought up. And**
> **after he [the bishop] has said the "Divine Grace" with a loud**
> **voice, the woman to be ordained bows her head.**[2]

Although the text is short, it is full of meaning. The time and the
place of the ordination indicate that we are dealing with a major
order. The ordination takes place in the sanctuary before the altar.
The doors of the screen are opened and the candidate is admitted
into the sanctuary itself. The ordination of the woman deacon takes
place during the liturgy of the eucharist and at a very solemn moment,
namely, after the sacred anaphora (offertory). So-called minor orders,
such as the lectorate and subdiaconate, were imparted outside the
sanctuary and not during the eucharist.

The reason for this most solemn of settings is that an ordination to
a major order is a public function in which the people take part. Not
only does the new minister need to be introduced, the people need to
express their approval of her election, according to ancient custom.
In the ordination to the diaconate as practiced in the Western Church
today, this is done through the calling forward of the candidates, their
presentation to the bishop, his acceptance of them, and the consent of
the people. In the Byzantine rite the same is done through the public
proclamation.

When the candidate stands before the bishop, the bishop makes a
public statement introducing the candidate by name and designating
him or her for the diaconate in a particular church. A short version
of the text read as follows:

> "Divine Grace, which always heals what is infirm and makes up
> for what is lacking, promotes [*name of person*] to be a Deacon

in [*name of place*]. Let us therefore pray that the grace of the Holy Spirit may descend on him/her."

The people reply, "Lord, have mercy on us!"[3]

The time, the place, the solemn declaration in the presence of the people and the clergy — all of it imparts a public character to the ordination. The intention is obviously for all to know that so-and-so will from now on be a deacon.[4]

After the public proclamation, the bishop turns to the woman to be ordained deacon. She bows her head to make it easier for him to impose his right hand.

First laying-on of hands

The ancient text continues in this way:

The bishop imposes his hand on her head, makes the sign of the cross on it three times, and prays:
[justification]
"Holy and Omnipotent Lord, through the birth of your Only Son our God from a Virgin according to the flesh, you have sanctified the female sex. You grant not only to men, but also to women the grace and coming down from above of the Holy Spirit."
[calling down the Holy Spirit]
"Please, Lord, look on this your maidservant and dedicate her to the work of your diaconate, and pour out into her the rich and abundant giving of your Holy Spirit."
[asking for perseverance]
"Preserve her so that she may always perform her ministry with orthodox faith and irreproachable conduct, according to what is pleasing to you.

For to you is due all glory and honor."

To appreciate the importance of this section, we need to remember the function of symbols in the sacramental order. Sacraments are, by definition, sacred signs. The Church has come to accept two aspects of the "sign" in each sacrament: the *matter* (an object or an action) and the *form* (the words that are spoken). In the case of holy orders, from time immemorial the imposition of hands has been considered as the *matter* of the sacrament, the invoking of the Spirit on the ordinand as the *form*.[5] These constitute the essence of the sacramental sign, by which everyone knows that this person has been truly ordained. By laying his hands on the head of the ordinand and by invocatory prayer the bishop imparts the sacrament.

In the ceremony we are studying here we find that the granting of the ministry to a woman is justified with an appeal to the fact that in Christ God has sanctified the female sex. The bishop knows what he is doing. Clearly and explicitly he calls down the Holy Spirit on the woman for the ministry of the diaconate. She is therefore *sacramentally* ordained. Note also that the laying-on of hands is performed for all the faithful to see, and the sacramental prayer is said aloud for the whole congregation to hear.

The Intercessions

The ancient ritual continues:

> **One of the other Deacons now starts a litany of intercessions: "for the salvation of our souls, for peace in the world, for our Archbishop, for our Emperor," etc. etc.**

Parallel rituals in other manuscripts give us a fuller description of this litany. Its relevance is that a special prayer for the ordinand was included.

> When [people] have responded: "Amen," one of the Deacons prays as follows: Let us pray the Lord in peace.

> For heavenly peace and the welfare of the whole universe, let us pray the Lord. [people's response] *Lord have mercy.*

For peace in the whole world, let us pray the Lord. *Lord have mercy.*

For [*name*], our Archbishop, for his priesthood, help, perseverance, peace, well-being, health and the works of his hands, let us pray the Lord. *Lord have mercy.*

For [*name*], the woman deacon, who has just been ordained, and for her salvation, let us pray the Lord. *Lord have mercy.*

That the most merciful Lord may give her a sincere and faultless diaconate, let us pray the Lord. *Lord have mercy.*

For our most devout and beloved-by-God emperor, [*name*], let us pray the Lord. *Lord have mercy.*[6]

The public prayer for the new woman deacon again confirms her sacramental ordination.

Second imposition of hands

The ancient ritual now introduces the second laying-on of hands, with its own traditional prayer. The text reads:

Meanwhile the Archbishop prays as follows keeping his hand on the head of the woman to be ordained:
[justification]
"Lord, Master, you do not reject women who dedicate themselves to you and who are willing, in a becoming way, to serve your Holy House, but admit them to the order of your ministers."
[calling down the Holy Spirit]
"Grant the gift of your Holy Spirit also to this your maidservant who wants to dedicate herself to you, and fulfil in her the work and the office of the ministry of the diaconate, as you have granted to Phoebe the grace of your diaconate, whom you had called to the work of this ministry."

[asking for perseverance]

"Grant her, Lord, that she may persevere without guilt in your Holy Temple, that she may carefully guard her behavior, especially her modesty and temperance.

Moreover, make your maidservant perfect, so that, when she stands before the judgment seat of your Christ, she may obtain the worthy fruit of her excellent conduct, through the mercy and humanity of your Only Son."

Thus the bishop performs the laying-on of hands and invokes the Holy Spirit a second time. Just like the first imposition, this action by itself would suffice to impart the sacrament. Only candidates for the three major orders — bishops, priests, and deacons — received a double imposition of hands. Perhaps the second imposition arose from a felt need to make absolutely sure that the candidate was validly ordained. Notice also that this second invocation of the Holy Spirit, which was known as the *ekphonese*, is spoken softly by the bishop.

Investiture

According to ancient practice, the newly ordained minister now receives the distinctive vestment by which she can be recognized as a deacon. Again we pick up the rubrics as narrated in the ancient ritual:

The Archbishop puts the stole of the diaconate around her neck, under her [woman's] veil, pulling the two extremities of the stole toward the front.

The bishop himself invests her with the distinctive vestment — *to diakonikon horarion* ['ωραριον], the diaconate stole — in a way that agrees with her veil, the *maphorion*. With this the main part of the ordination rite has been completed.

Now the central eucharistic functions begin with the various rites characteristic of the Byzantine liturgy. One of the priests and the deacon carry the paten and chalice in procession around the church. The bread and the wine on the altar are incensed. The deacon intones another litany of intercessions. There follow further ceremonies and prayers, including the prayer of consecration and the epiclesis, the calling down of the Holy Spirit on the sacred bread and wine, and another litany of intercessions. As in the Latin rite, the Our Father is said and the bread is broken.

In the Byzantine rite, the unleavened bread is square, with a large cross in the middle. The four corners are marked as IC (Jesus), XC (Christ), NI and KA (which together mean "victory"). The bishop breaks the bread into four parts. He places the portion marked IC into the chalice, XC is earmarked for himself and for the priests and deacons, and the two remaining portions, NI and KA, are divided into small portions and placed into the chalice for the ordinary communicants.

It is now time for communion.

Distributing communion

It is here that the ordination ritual picks up the thread again. This is necessary because a deacon distributes holy communion. Deacons themselves receive communion directly from the bishop:

When [at the time of communion] the newly ordained has taken part of the precious body and blood, the Archbishop hands her the holy vessel. She accepts it and, without distributing it to others, puts it back on the holy table [the altar].

The bishop takes the consecrated bread allocated to the assistant ministers and distributes it to the priests and deacons. They, each in turn, kiss the hand with which he gives them the holy bread and say, "Impart unto me, Master, the precious and holy Body of our Lord and God and Savior Jesus Christ." The bishop puts the consecrated bread on their hand, with words that mention the recipient by name: "To you, deacon so-and-so, is imparted the precious, and holy, and immaculate Body of our Lord and God and Savior Jesus Christ, unto forgiveness of your sins and unto life eternal." The bishop then partakes of the consecrated bread himself.

The bishop then takes communion from the chalice, sipping three times, and praying: "The precious and holy Blood of our Lord and God and Savior Jesus Christ is imparted unto me, the servant of God, [*mentioning his own name*], unto forgiveness of my sins and unto life eternal. Amen." He then gives the chalice to the priests and deacons, using a similar formula and again mentioning the recipient by name: "Unto you, the servant of God, deacon [*name*], is imparted the precious and holy Blood of our Lord and God and Savior Jesus Christ, unto forgiveness of your sins and unto life eternal." Of course, when there were many priests and deacons, one of the priests would assist the bishop in handing communion to the clergy.

Did the newly ordained woman deacon receive communion with the clergy? The answer is yes, as is clear from this explicit statement in one of the ordination rituals:

At the time of the partaking of the sacred mysteries, she shares of the divine body and blood with the deacons.[7]

It should be noted that this is highly significant. The new woman deacon was present in the sanctuary with the other clergy, for the holy doors of the iconostasis were still closed. She was given the host on her hand by the bishop as her male colleagues were. And she drank from the chalice as they did.

Now a special rite was added. For it was customary for a new male deacon to be introduced to his task by making him share in the distribution of holy communion to the laity:

The Archbishop hands her the holy vessel. She accepts it and, without distributing it to others, puts it back on the holy table [the altar].

In church it was the male deacons who distributed communion to the faithful. But to show that, in principle, the woman deacon too received the same commission, the bishop handed her the chalice which contained the consecrated bread and wine, and she herself put it back onto the altar. This was the end of the woman's ordination to the diaconate.

The doors of the screen were now opened and the male deacon(s) went out to give communion to the faithful. Ministers distributed communion by scooping a small particle of bread soaked in wine from the chalice with a little spoon and giving it to people on the tongue. They came forward, with their hands folded before the chest, and received communion on the tongue. The communicant would then kiss the chalice and withdraw. The liturgy concluded with the purification of the sacred vessels, prayers, and the solemn blessing.

Conclusion

The ordination rite of a woman deacon, set within the framework of a full Byzantine celebration of the eucharist, shows clearly that women deacons did receive the full sacramental holy order of the diaconate.

We recall the words of the Council of Trent: "If anyone says that, through sacred ordination, the Holy Spirit is not given, and that therefore the bishop says in vain: 'Receive the Holy Spirit,' or that through this ordination the character [of holy orders] is not imprinted... *Let him be anathema.*"[8]

5

The ritual for men and women compared

NO ONE DOUBTS that male deacons received a true and valid sacramental ordination. It will be useful, therefore, to compare the rituals for the ordination of men and women to the diaconate. What differences, if any, were there? Full rituals for both the ordination of male and female candidates to the diaconate are found in all the ancient manuscripts listed in chapter 3. But our immediate source, as in the previous chapter, will be the Bessarion Codex, which has been preserved in the Greek monastery at Grottaferrata.

In all the manuscripts concerned, the ritual for ordaining women deacons comes either immediately after or before the one for ordaining male deacons. But since our primary purpose here is to compare the two rituals, I will print them side by side in my own, rather literal translation from the Greek, so that sameness or difference can be easily spotted. Since many details of the text will be discussed at length in the chapters that follow, I will limit my observations to rather short statements of fact.

Public election of the candidate

The ordination of deacons	*Prayer at the ordination of a deaconess*
After the sacred offertory, the doors [of the sanctuary] are opened and before the deacon starts the litany "All Saints," the man who is to be ordained deacon is brought before the archbishop. And when the "Divine Grace" statement has been said, the ordinand kneels on his right knee.	After the sacred offertory, the doors [of the sanctuary] are opened and, before the [officiating] deacon starts the litany "All Saints," the woman who is to be ordained deacon is brought up. And after he [the bishop] has said the "Divine Grace" with a loud voice, the woman to be ordained bows her head.

We notice that the ordination of both male and female deacon takes place during the liturgy of the eucharist and at a very solemn moment, namely, after the sacred anaphora (offertory). The bishop proclaims the "Divine Grace" statement for both the man and the woman.

When the laying-on of hands starts, the two candidates assume a slightly different posture. The male deacon-to-be kneels, bending his right knee. The woman deacon-to-be bows her head. The bishop imposes his hand on either of them. The difference in posture is due to the dress they wear. The man probably leans with his head on the altar. Probably so does she.

First laying-on of hands

Male ordinand

The archbishop puts the sign of the cross on his forehead three times, keeps his hand imposed on his head and prays:

[justification]
"Lord our God, in your providence you send the working and abundance of your Holy Spirit on those who through your inscrutable power are constituted liturgical ministers to serve your immaculate mysteries."

[calling down the Holy Spirit]
"Please, preserve, Lord, this man whom you want me to promote to the ministry of the diaconate, in all seriousness and strictness of good behavior, that he may guard the mystery of faith with a pure conscience. And give him grace which you have given to Stephen your first martyr."

[asking for perseverance]
"And after having called him to the work of your ministry, in your good pleasure

Female ordinand

The bishop imposes his hand on her head, makes the sign of the cross on it three times, and prays:

[justification]
"Holy and Omnipotent Lord, through the birth of your Only Son our God from a Virgin according to the flesh, you have sanctified the female sex. You grant not only to men, but also to women the grace and coming (from above) of the Holy Spirit."

[calling down the Holy Spirit]
"Please, Lord, look on this your maid-servant and dedicate her to the work of your diaconate, and pour out into her the rich and abundant giving of your Holy Spirit."

[asking for perseverance]
"Preserve her so that she may always perform her ministry with orthodox faith

make him worthy to perform the degree [of responsibility] you entrust to him. For those who perform it well, will acquire for themselves a high degree. Make your servant perfect, for yours are the kingdom and the power."

and irreproachable conduct, according to what is pleasing to you.

For to you is due all glory and honor."

Let us start by observing that the mention of "archbishop" in the case of the man, and "bishop" for the woman candidate is pure coincidence. Usually the rituals that mention "archbishop" were copied from an *euchologion* used by an archbishop, those that mention "bishop" from an *euchologion* in the possession of a bishop. Here, in the case of the ritual for women deacons, what begins as "bishop" turns into "archbishop" later.

The crucial fact is, of course, that the bishop lays his hands on the head of either ordinand, and by invoking the Holy Spirit for the ministry of the diaconate, the bishop imparts the sacrament to both.

There are slight differences in the words used, to accommodate the special situation of the man and the woman. But the structure of the ordination prayer is the same for both. The key words of "Holy Spirit," "ministry," and "diaconate" are applied to both.

The Intercessions

Male ordinand	*Female ordinand*
The archdeacon now makes the intercessions, as stated before.	After the "Amen," one of the [officiating] deacons now makes the usual intercessions.

We know from parallel rituals in other manuscripts that special prayer for the ordinands were included. One of the prayers we find was "For so-and-so the deaconess, who has just been ordained, and for her salvation, let us pray the Lord. That the most merciful Lord may give her a sincere and faultless diaconate, let us pray the Lord."[1] Such intercessions are said both for an ordained man and an ordained woman, using the same formula.

Second laying-on of hands

Male ordinand

Meanwhile the archbishop, keeping his hand on the head of the ordinand, prays as follows:

[justification]
"God, our Savior, with incorruptible voice you have foretold it, you announced that he would be first who would perform the ministry of the diaconate, as is written in your holy Gospel: 'Who ever wants to be first among you, must be your servant [*diakonos*],'"

[calling down the Holy Spirit]
"Please, Lord of all, fill this servant of yours whom you have made worthy to enter the ministry [*leitourgia*] of deacon, through the life-giving coming of your Holy Spirit with all faith, charity, power and holiness."

[asking for perseverance]
"Now, Lord, look upon this man. For grace is given to those you deem worthy, not by the imposition of my hands, but by the visitation of your rich mercy, so that, purified from sin, he may on that fearful day of your judgment be presented to you without guilt, and receive the reward of your unfailing promise.

For you are our God, of mercy and salvation, and to you we give glory, Father, Son, and Holy Spirit."

Female ordinand

Meanwhile the archbishop, keeping his hand on the head of the woman to be ordained, prays as follows:

[justification]
"Lord, Master, you do not reject women who dedicate themselves to you and who are willing, in a becoming way, to serve your Holy House, but admit them to the order of your ministers [*leitourgôn*]."

[calling down the Holy Spirit]
"Grant the gift of your Holy Spirit also to this your maidservant who wants to dedicate herself to you, and fulfil in her the work and the office of the ministry [*leitourgia*] of the diaconate, as you have granted to Phoebe the grace of your diaconate, whom you had called to the work of this ministry [*leitourgia*]."

[asking for perseverance]
"Grant her, Lord, that she may persevere without guilt in your Holy Temple, that she may carefully guard her behavior, especially her prudence and chastity. Moreover, make your maidservant perfect, so that, when she stands before the judgment seat of your Christ, she may obtain the worthy reward of her good conduct, through the mercy and generosity of your Only Son."

We have noted before that this second laying-on of hands and the accompanying invocation of the Holy Spirit would by itself suffice to impart the sacrament. Only candidates for the three major orders — bishops, priests, and deacons — received a *double* imposition of hands. Here we see that it was given to both the male and female candidate.

Again the ordination prayer is substantially identical. For the man, the deacon Stephen is held out as the model, for the woman the deacon Phoebe fulfils this role.

Investiture

Male ordinand	*Female ordinand*
The archbishop takes away the [man's] scarf from the ordinand and lays a stole [on his shoulders]. He kisses him and hands him the holy fan and makes him fan the holy gifts when they are exposed on the [altar] table.	The archbishop puts the stole of the diaconate around her neck, under her [woman's] veil, arranging the two extremities of the stole toward the front.

Both the male and the female deacon receive the stole as their official vestment. The male deacon, one of whose future tasks it will be to assist at the altar during the eucharist, is handed the sacred fan and made to wave it over the gifts for the first time.

Distributing communion

Male ordinand	*Female ordinand*
When [at the time of communion] the newly ordained has taken part of the sacred body and precious blood, the archbishop hands him the chalice. He in turn makes all those who approach him take part in the sacred blood.	When [at the time of communion] the newly ordained has taken part of the sacred body and precious blood, the archbishop hands her the chalice. She accepts it and puts it on the holy table [the altar].

Both the male and the female deacon are handed the chalice by the bishop. According to Byzantine practice, this chalice contains parts of the consecrated bread immersed in the consecrated wine. By holding the chalice in their hands both the male and female deacon accept the task of distributing communion. Since male deacons assisted at the eucharist in church, the male deacon starts to distribute at his ordination. Female deacons took communion to the sick.

Assessment

Most scholars consider the close parallel between the two ordination rites a strong argument for accepting women's diaconate as having been as much a sacrament as the diaconate of men. "It cannot be denied that the ordination ritual puts women deacons and male deacons on entirely the same level."[2]

This is also the considered opinion of the Orthodox scholar Kallistos Ware. He wrote classic books such as *The Orthodox Church* and *The Orthodox Way.* He co-authored and co-translated into English a number of important Orthodox liturgical and spiritual texts, including a multivolume edition of the Orthodox classic collection of spiritual writings, *The Philokalia.*[3] Since 1966, he has been Spalding Lecturer in Eastern Orthodox Studies at Oxford, becoming a Fellow of Pembroke College, Oxford in 1970. In 1982, he was consecrated titular bishop of Diokleia and appointed assistant bishop in the Orthodox Archdiocese of Thyateira and Great Britain, under the Ecumenical Patriarchate. Bishop Kallistos judges women deacons to have been truly ordained:

> The order of deaconess seems definitely to have been considered an "ordained" ministry during early centuries in at any rate the Christian East. . . . Some Orthodox writers regard deaconesses as having been a "lay" ministry. There are strong reasons for rejecting this view. In the Byzantine rite the liturgical office for the laying-on of hands for the deaconess is exactly parallel to that for the deacon; and so on the principle *lex orandi, lex credendi* — the Church's worshipping practice is a sure indication of its faith — it follows that the deaconess receives, as does the deacon, a genuine sacramental ordination: not just a χειροθεσια but a χειροτονια.[4]

He repeated his opinion in an interview with *St. Nina Quarterly* in 1997:

> The order of deaconess was never abolished, it merely fell into disuse. On my understanding of the evidence, they were

regarded as ordained persons on an equal footing as the male deacons. There is some dispute in the Orthodox world about that, but my reading of the evidence is quite clear — that they have received not just a blessing but an ordination.[5]

Critics

Not everyone agrees with this assessment, though it is at present shared by a majority of scholars. Champion of the opposition is, without any doubt, the French liturgist Aimé-Georges Martimort. Martimort was founder of the Center for Pastoral Liturgy in Paris and its director from 1946 to 1964. Later he was director of the Catholic Institute of Toulouse. He wrote a number of liturgical works, some of which are available in English: *In Remembrance of Me* (1958), *The Eucharist* (1971), and *The Church at Prayer* (1992), of which he was the editor. He gave his services as a liturgical expert to the Preparatory Commission of the Second Vatican Council. He also served as consultor to the Congregation for Divine Worship from before the Second Vatican Council until the time of his death. Aimé-Georges Martimort died in Toulouse on January 20, 2000.

In 1982 Martimort wrote an important book, *Les diaconesses: Essai historique*. It was published in English as *Deaconesses: An Historical Study* (San Francisco, 1986). With regard to women deacons in the Byzantine realm, Martimort judged their ministry to have been purely a minor order, not part of the sacrament of holy orders: "However solemn may have been the ritual by which she was initiated into her ministry, however much it may have resembled the ritual for the ordination of a deacon, a deaconess in the Byzantine rite was in no wise a female deacon. She exercised a totally different ministry from that of the deacons."[6] And here is a list of his arguments:

- Talking about "sacrament" in those early centuries is an anachronism.

- Women deacons did not serve at the altar during the eucharistic service, and they did not distribute communion.

- The stole received by the woman deacon was not a true diaconate stole.

- The laying-on of hands does not necessarily mean ordination. Subdeacons and readers too were installed with an imposition of hands.

- Women deacons were only nuns. Their so-called "ordination" was just a solemn blessing.

- The liturgical moment and the place of women's ordination bear no real significance.

- The diaconate of women lacked continuity going back to apostolic times.

- It was a local, rare, and ambiguous phenomenon.

- Women *could not* have been given the sacrament of holy orders because this sacrament is restricted to men.

Martimort's work has been hailed by some as "a masterpiece of research" (in *The Priest*), "the last word" (in the *Homiletic and Pastoral Review*), and "the definitive work on the subject" (in *The Diaconate*). Opponents of the ordination of women cite Martimort as their authority. We will therefore make him their spokesman and consider his objections one by one. Discussing them will provide a welcome opportunity of further study. It will put our own assessment to the test and reveal the ancient ordination rite in more detail.

6

Is talk of "sacrament" an anachronism?

WEBSTER'S DICTIONARY defines an anachronism as "a chronological misplacing of persons, events, objects or customs in regard to each other." For instance, if I read in a book, "Jesus phoned St. Andrew and asked him to hop on the Underground and meet him over a hamburger at McDonald's in Bethesda," I know it is fiction. There were no telephones, underground trains, hamburgers, or fast-food shops in Jerusalem during Jesus' time. Are we making the same mistake when we judge women's diaconate to have been a true sacrament? Martimort says, "With regard to the question of whether or not the ordination of deaconesses had any sacramental value, it is evident that no decisive theological conclusion can be reached ... without falling into a serious anachronism."[1]

A letter from my mailbag, in response to an article I wrote, explains the problem in more detail:[2]

> Your use of the word *sacrament* in the context of the early women's diaconate is an anachronism. The distinction between "a sacrament" and "a sacramental" arose only in the 12th century. Hugo of St. Victor (1096–1141) was the first to contrast "the minor sacraments" and "the sacraments through which our salvation is mainly found." Peter Lombard (1100–1160) coined the term "sacramentals" in opposition to the "seven sacraments." You may not apply our present theological terminology to the Byzantine Church of the first millennium.[3]

This worry has also been expressed in print.[4] On closer examination it turns out to be unfounded. But first we must consider more at length the history of our Christian "sacramental order."

Mystery and sign

There is more to life than just chemistry and physics. God is the tremendous mystery hidden behind everything we can see, hear, and touch. The people and things that surround us can become symbols of that deeper all-pervasive presence. Then they become windows to what is invisible. They point to reality beyond themselves. For instance, a volcano that erupts presents a picture of unimaginable force. It becomes a *symbol* for us if we, as it were, look through it and see the inexhaustible mysterious force behind the universe. Experiencing our mother's love, we may suddenly grasp that in her we are touching love itself, another aspect of our mysterious human existence. Our mother's love has then been made transparent. Apart from its own value, it assumes a deeper meaning. It has been discovered to be a symbol pointing beyond itself. This is the basis for all religion.

It is natural for us to give the high points of our existence a festive form charged with significance. When someone is born or reaches puberty or gets married or dies, we mark the event by a celebration which contrasts with the dullness of everyday life. In cultures all over the world symbols have been created that express the deeper meaning of such moments: rituals, customs, special dresses, specific food and drink. Through these symbols, which are often religious in origin, we reach out to what lies beyond us and celebrate the mystery of our existence. In fact, we cannot deal with the most important realities in our life without signs and symbols.

Enter Jesus Christ. He was, in his own person, the deepest religious symbol par excellence. Scripture calls him the "reflection of the Father's glory," "the imprint of the Father's being" (Hebrews 1:3), "image of the invisible God" (Colossians 1:15). Jesus Christ showed us, in his humanity, what God is like. Whoever saw him, saw the Father (John 14:7–9). Who heard his words, heard the Father speak (John 7:16). Everything Jesus did was a visible, audible, tangible expression of God's love for us. Jesus was, therefore, the living sign of God among us; or, to use the proper theological term, he was *the sacrament* of God meeting us, speaking to us, forgiving us, healing us, making us God's adopted children. For "sacrament" means "sign."

We Christians believe that in Jesus Christ religion attained a new dimension. Although natural religious symbols still preserve their meaning, after Christ's coming a whole new set of religious symbols was created that continue Christ's presence. It is known as *the sacramental order.* The community of believers, which we call the Church, is the overriding sacrament: it is the lasting sign of Christ surrounding us and holding us. In and through his community Christ speaks to us, saves us, heals us, fulfils our spiritual needs.

Sacrament is, therefore, a typically Christian term. And although all actions of the community of believers somehow take place within the sacramental order, in the course of time certain specific symbols were selected to become "sacraments" in a very special way. The central sign of all was shaped very personally by Jesus Christ himself on the night before he died. He used the typically human custom of eating together as a sign to manifest and to bring about his unity with us. He took bread and wine and said, "This is my body for you...This is my blood of the new covenant." But it is not only in the *eucharist,* the great sacrament of his presence, that he acts upon us. When a child is born or a person received into the Church, we celebrate *baptism* in Christ. We mark a person through *confirmation* for the moment of Christian maturity. When a man and a woman *marry* each other, their shared life becomes a lasting sign of Christ's presence. The imparting of pastoral responsibility through *ordination* is another gesture of Christ. When we fall and sin, he is there for us in the sacrament of *penance.* And in that critical moment of our lives when we are gravely ill, he is with us in the *anointing of the sick.*

Since the twelfth century these signs have been known as the seven sacraments. The growth of specialist language about this was unavoidable.[5]

Making sense of theological terminology

Years ago, in a popular TV program Esther Rantzen used to award the weekly prize for "bureaucratic gobbledegook." One gem I remember was the letter from a municipal planning department: "Considering inadequate reciprocal first-degree fireproof-consistent anti-corrosive adhesion treatment as stipulated in Amended County Building Regulations sect. IV art. 5b, your application signaling preliminary intent fails to meet minimal municipal safety standards requirements." Now we must note that the text may sound gobbledegook to us, while making perfect sense to a building engineer. Specialists who try to be precise invent their own language. The same has happened in theology. Theologians have created a distinct academic dialect. What scholars are saying when speaking of holy orders, sacrament, and ordination can be fully understood by us only when we take the trouble to absorb their vocabulary.

It took a long time for the precise meaning of the term "sacrament" to be fully worked out. St. Augustine (354–430) offered the first technical definition of a sacrament as "a visible sign of invisible grace." Since some people dismissed sacraments as "*only* signs without effect," St. Thomas Aquinas explained that they *cause* grace insofar as they signify it.[6] For example, when someone is baptized, that person's sins are truly forgiven and he or she becomes an adopted child of God. This explanation was repeated by the Council of Trent in 1547, which declared that the seven sacraments "contain" the grace which they signify and produce their effect not just by the faith of the recipient but by God whose power is attached to the symbol itself.[7]

In other words, the seven sacraments are *effective* symbols. The tearing up of a contract does not only *signify* the end of mutual obligations, it brings it about. When the queen knights a person by laying a sword on his left shoulder, she changes his status in law. Catholics believe that, on the full sacramental level, what is symbolized really happens. The priest gives the absolution — sins are truly forgiven. In the eucharist Christ is really present under the species of bread and wine. When a bishop ordains a priest, the priest is consecrated to make Christ present in the ministry of teaching, healing, presiding, gathering.

The concern to safeguard the intrinsic value of the sacrament led theologians to distinguish three elements: the sign itself (*sacramentum tantum*), the grace it conveys (*res tantum*), and its intrinsic value (*res et sacramentum*). When hosts are consecrated in the eucharist, they achieve their purpose of uniting the faithful to Christ when they are received, with faith, in holy communion. But what happens to the hosts that remain? If they had a purely transitory function, they could be simply disposed of after Mass — as indeed happens in some Protestant churches. But the Catholic tradition has come to regard these hosts as somehow permanently linked to Christ, which is expressed by Catholic belief in the "Real Presence." So the hosts are kept in a tabernacle. They can be used later to bring the viaticum to the sick. They retain some lasting intrinsic link to God.

In three sacraments, baptism, confirmation, and holy orders, this lasting intrinsic link is called "character." Once a person is baptized, he or she is never baptized again, even if the person gave up his or her beliefs and Christian practice for many years, because the link to Christ acquired through the original baptism remains. Once a person is ordained to be a deacon, priest, or bishop, the commission to ministry is there to stay. The Greek word *character* means a "seal." The image was derived from the seal branded into the flesh of a slave or a soldier by which that person was forever identified as belonging to a particular master. Theologians loved to talk of "an indelible mark" branded into the soul by these sacraments, but this goes over the top. The meaning is simply that these sacraments have a lasting effect. In other words, once performed, the sign retains its value and should not be repeated. It was for that purpose that the Council of Trent declared it to be heresy "if anyone says that the Holy Spirit is not given through sacred ordination, or that it is in vain that bishops say, 'Receive the Holy Spirit,' or that through ordination no character is imprinted, or that he who has once been ordained a priest, can be a lay person again."[8]

The ordination of the woman deacon should be seen in this light. Even though women can perform so many services in the Church without ordination, the seal of the Holy Spirit on their ministry gives it a deeper dimension:

> The ministry of the diaconate, also of women, is an ecclesial function. From a theological point of view, it should be transmitted through sacramental ordination. Sacramental ordination is not a personal privilege, nor promotion to higher spirituality nor an ontological change of personality.
>
> By sacramental ordination the community with its leaders expresses that this task that transcends the power of any individual can only be undertaken through the power of the Spirit. "Woe to me if I do not proclaim the Gospel — woe to me if I do not live up to my ministry!" This human "woe to me!" is met by the "success to you!" in the calling down of the Holy Spirit at ordination.[9]

Valid sacrament or not?

In the practice of the Church the question has often arisen as to whether a particular action had been a true sacrament or not. The Synod of Arles in France decided in 314 that converts from the Donatist sect should be asked if they had been baptized in the name of the Father, Son, and Holy Spirit. If they had, their baptism had been valid and they should not be rebaptized. But the Council of Nicea decreed eleven years later that the baptism of the followers of Paul of Samosata, the heretical bishop of Antioch in Syria, was not valid. The reason was that the Paulicians considered Jesus to be a human being who became divine only gradually. Paulicians had to be rebaptized.

Then how to determine what the minimum conditions for a particular sacrament are?

St. Augustine had already noted that baptism requires "the word and a material substance." He meant: it requires the formula "I baptize you" and immersion in water.[10] Other Fathers of the Church noted the same duality. It was the medieval theologians, however, who worked this out in great detail. For they often were also church lawyers by profession. They loved to define the exact conditions of a sacrament's validity. And they drew their terminology from Greek philosophy, which had been rediscovered by the universities of the time.

Any object was deemed to consist of two components: matter and form. A cat, for instance, was thought to be composed of two distinct elements, its body and its inner life, its "soul." Take away the cat's soul, and only a corpse is left. Adam was just a clay model (*matter*) until God blew the human soul (*form*) into his nostrils (Genesis 2:7). In the same way, each sacrament has its *matter* and its *form,* both of which are essential for its validity. In the case of baptism, the matter is washing in water, the form the baptismal words "I baptize you in the name of the Father, the Son, and the Holy Spirit," or an equivalent phrase. With regard to each and every sacrament, they determined matter and form by observing how the Church actually administered the sacraments and what had been said about them in earlier tradition.

Now the "form" is identical to the words that accompany the material sign. Although standard formulas are often used, this need not be the case. There have been different ways of expressing baptism. The Trinitarian formula has been widespread. However, there is also ancient evidence for the use of "I baptize you in the name of Jesus" (Acts 2:38; 8:12, 16; 10:48; 19:5).[11] Different *forms* have been used for the eucharist, for penance, and for confirmation. What counts is the intention of the person administering the sacrament. His or her intention gives inner life to the form. But what happens if the person administering the sacrament does not fully understand the form? What if she is an uneducated mother baptizing her dying baby? The theologians replied that the "minister" must at least have the intention of "doing what the Church does."

Intention and form are closely related. When Leo XIII declared Anglican orders invalid, he did so not only on account of defects in the ordination prayer (the "form"), but also because he judged the intention of some crucial bishops in the chain of succession to have been insufficient. For, being influenced by Protestant ideas, they did not want to ordain sacrificial priests with a view to offering the eucharist. He judged this sufficient to invalidate the sacrament, for the words they used no longer meant what the Church meant by them.[12]

Notice also the difference between an action being "licit" or "valid." A bishop, for instance, can impart a valid priestly ordination to a boy who is only sixteen years old. But the ordination would be illicit, since church law prescribes the minimum age to be twenty-four. It is the validity question that predominates in theology.

And what about "sacramentals"?

The community of believers has created many smaller symbolic actions which are not sacraments (therefore not strictly sacramental), yet somehow belong to the wider sacramental (i.e., symbolic) order of Christian life. They are, unfortunately, called the "sacramentals." Perplexity can easily arise from the same word being used in different senses. In English, "sacramental" as an adjective means "belonging to a sacrament"; "a sacramental," as a noun, means "belonging *only* to the wider sacramental order." Confused? You may well be. A theologian may say, "Yes. Confirmation is sacramental (*adjective*). But blessing holy water is only *a* sacramental (*noun*)." He or she would mean that confirmation is a true sacrament, but blessing holy water is not.

Such subtle differences exist in other contexts. A similar shift of meaning can be seen in the words "mobile" and "*a* mobile" (a hand-held phone). Compare: "I'm sick in bed and not mobile. But I have a mobile." Or think of "ordinary" and "*an* ordinary" (church parlance for the bishop of a diocese): "It is not ordinary for an ordinary to drive his own car." Someone can be "*a* secular" (church parlance for a diocesan priest) without being secular (i.e., worldly) in his lifestyle!

Examples of sacramentals are marking oneself with holy water when entering a church building; the blessing of the throat on St. Blaise's feast; dedicating a home to the Sacred Heart; exorcism;

consecrating a church or chapel; the installation of readers and ministers of holy communion.

It makes a huge difference whether a theologian judges the ancient diaconate of women to have been "sacramental" (i.e., a full, true sacrament), or "only *a* sacramental" (i.e., no more than a blessing). Be forewarned!

Back to the "anachronism" objection

Anachronism involves placing persons, events, or objects in the wrong time. If I say, "Jesus took a taxi to the Jerusalem railway station," I am committing an anachronism. But what if I say, "Jesus instituted the sacraments"? This phrase was actually used by the Council of Trent in 1563. But Jesus did not know the word "sacrament," you may object. True. But he was very much aware of the symbolism of the actions he established, such as baptism and the eucharist. The same applied to the Byzantine bishops who ordained women deacons. They did not know the word "sacrament," but they understood its substance. The circumstance that people at a particular time did not have a clear *term* for an object or an event, or did not define it theologically as we do today, does not disprove the *reality* of that object or event.

In 1995 the archeologist David Soren of Arizona University discovered a cemetery for children dated to around 450. All the children had died from a mysterious disease. Soren correlated this event with evidence of an epidemic sweeping through that part of Italy at about the same time. Some indications pointed to malaria as the culprit. Then Robert Sellares of the University of Manchester identified the genes of falciparum malaria in the bones of one of the children. This fatal form of malaria must have been transported from Africa to Italy and caused an epidemic. The contemporaries realized that something terrible had hit them, but they could not give it an exact name. In 467 the Roman writer Sidonius described the illness with symptoms that match malaria, but he simply called it a "fever," a "pestilence." Now it is perfectly legitimate *for us* to say that those children died of falciparum malaria, even though it is a term Romans would not have recognized.

The Hittite language had no word for "covenant" or "treaty," and certainly not for "vassal treaty." Hittites would vaguely speak of "the oath" or "swearing a pledge." Yet stone tablets found at Bogazköj in Turkey contained the complete texts of at least nineteen "vassal treaties," imposed by Hittite emperors on the kings of Amurru, Ugarit, Kizuwatna, and other countries during the second millennium BC. All these treaties display the characteristic structure of the names of the partners, prologue, main stipulation of loyalty, covenant obligations, and the invocation of blessings and curses.[13] Is speaking of the Hittite vassal treaties an anachronism?

From the ritual of the ordination rite it is clear that ordaining a deacon, whether man or woman, was a very holy and solemn act, through which the power of the Holy Spirit was bestowed on the ordinand for a sacred task. Here is clear evidence of the sacramental order of sacred symbols through which Christ is present to his community. Pseudo-Dionysius (around AD 500) says that only three kinds of leaders belong to the "order of sacred ministers" [τάξις των 'ιερουργων]: those who purify (deacons), those who enlighten (priests), and those who perfect (bishops).[14]

Such considerations make it clear that "both in the West and the East there were equivalent notions to sacramentality.... There existed a widely received theology that understood *cheirotonia* or *cheirothesia* (the imposition of hands) as the act that mediated the empowerment and the grace of the Holy Spirit on the ordinand. It clearly entails the substance of 'sacrament' even if the word is not used."[15] "From at least AD 400 a clear distinction between major and minor orders began to emerge.... Ordination is understood in terms of what we today would call a sacrament."[16]

In other words, Byzantine Christians recognized the ordination to the diaconate as a sacrament, just as baptism, confession, the eucharist, and extreme unction were sacraments for them, even if they used other terms. Martimort is mistaken calling talk of sacrament an anachronism in this case.

7

Excluded from "any sacred service"?

MARTIMORT asserts that "women deacons were prohibited from any liturgical role."[1] He states that the ordination prayers show a different function for the male and female deacon:

> Deacons were to be "servants of Christ and stewards of the mysteries of God" (1 Cor. 4:1). They were to "hold the mystery of faith with a clear conscience" (1 Tim. 3:9). In this the commentators have always seen a clear reference to the ministry of distributing Communion from the chalice. Moreover, immediately after his ordination, the deacon proceeded immediately to carry out this and other tasks proper to his ministry: he shook the *rhipidion,* or fan intended to keep flies away, which was given to him by the bishop; he gave out the Precious Blood to the faithful in Communion; and he also chanted the final litany.
>
> The deaconess, however, was to "persevere without reproach in God's holy temples"; she was to "apply herself to household government," which was the proper work precisely of the *hegumenē* [superior] of a convent of contemplative nuns but implied no other outside work or service; certainly it implied no liturgical role.[2]

Martimort also finds an essential difference in the posture of the candidates, since the woman ordinand bows her head, while the man genuflects on one knee:

> The fact that the deaconess bowed her head and was not permitted to genuflect was, according to Pseudo-Dionysius, the sign that her role was not considered to be equivalent to that of the

deacon; further, the deacon genuflected on one knee, the priest on two, and these gestures were precisely intended to signify differences of order. If, during her ordination, the deaconess did not rest her head against the altar, it was because, in fact, she received no power pertaining to the altar and, indeed, did not even have access to the altar.[3]

Martimort concludes from this that "a deaconess in the Byzantine rite was in no wise a female deacon. She exercised a totally different ministry from that of the deacon."[4]

His objections look impressive at first sight and might persuade unwary readers. Yes, it is a fact that, because of the cultural beliefs of the time, women were not admitted to priestly ordination. It is also true that it was the male deacon, not the woman deacon, who assisted the bishop or priest at the eucharist. But a closer examination reveals that, in spite of these restrictions, women *were* ordained to the full diaconate, which included access to the altar.

Limits imposed because of gender

Cultural and theological prejudices of the time could not envisage women performing priestly roles. The question came up only when women were given priestly functions among the Collyridians, and among members of other Christian sects. For traditional Christians it was unthinkable for a woman to preside over the eucharist because no woman could have authority over men. Such a thing would offend "nature and [Roman] law" (Augustine).[5] Women are "a feeble race, untrustworthy and of mediocre intelligence" (Epiphanius).[6] Women are not "created in God's image" (Tertullian, Ambrosiaster).[7] And, had Paul for such reasons not forbidden women to speak in the assembly (John Chrysostom)?[8] In a document known as the *Apostolic Constitutions* (AD 380) the reasons are set out in this fashion:

> The man is the head of the woman, and it is the man who is chosen to be ordained for the priesthood ['ιεροσυνη]. Therefore it is not correct to subvert the order of creation, and reduce the

origin to the derived parts of the body. In fact, the woman is the body of the man, taken from his side, and subject to him. She was separated from him for the procreation of children. For [God] says: "He [the man] shall rule over you [the woman]." For the origin of the woman is the man, and therefore her head. And if, in the foregoing constitutions we have not permitted them to teach, how will any one allow them, contrary to nature, to perform the office of a priest ['ιερατευσαι]? For to ordain women priests ['ιερειας] to female deities is one of the ignorant practices of the pagans, not one of the laws of Christ.[9]

In chapter 13 we will have occasion to discuss more fully this prejudice against ordaining women to the priesthood. For our purpose here it suffices to note that the diaconate ordination did not ordain women to the *priesthood.* So what? Male deacons too, though some might at a later stage move on to priestly ordination, were *only deacons,* and most remained in that separate function all their lives. The same *Apostolic Constitutions* describe the difference in unmistakable terms. "A deacon does not bless [any object], does not give the blessing [at the eucharist], but receives it from the bishop and priest. He does not baptize, he does not offer [the eucharist]; but when a bishop or presbyter has offered [it], he distributes [communion] to the people, not as a priest ['ιερευς], but as one that ministers to the priests."[10]

In other words: a deacon is only a deacon, whether man or woman. But a prejudice against women *as priests* does not prove women could not be deacons.

Then what about serving at the altar?

Indeed, there *was* a difference in the tasks entrusted to male and female deacons. It was the male deacon who assisted the bishop (or priest) at every stage of the eucharistic worship. He sang litanies, he prepared the gifts, he stood next to the presiding celebrant during the prayers of consecration, he helped in distributing holy communion.

This different task is reflected in one or two minor aspects of the male deacon's ordination: he is given the *rhipidion,* the sacred "fan," and operates it, while the woman deacon does not. He distributes communion, while the woman deacon puts back the chalice. But does the difference in *task* establish a difference in the sacramental status of men and women deacons?

Frederick McManus, the distinguished American liturgical canonist, has remarked that bishops too had many different tasks in history. Some were prince bishops (in the Middle Ages). Today, some are administrator bishops and financier bishops (in the Vatican Curia). Some are nuncios to governments. "A historian of the twenty-fifth century might conclude, from a reading of the modern Roman Pontifical, that such bishops never existed because these functions are not mentioned in the consecratory prayers." And are bishops ordained for a different task not validly ordained? Martimort's reasoning is therefore invalid.[11]

Further, why was it the male deacon who assisted the celebrating bishop or priest at the altar, and not the woman? Martimort suggests it was the principle to keep women away from the altar, which, again presumably, she was not holy enough to touch. Instead, there was an obvious, practical reason.

Most eucharistic actions, as we have seen in chapter 4, took place behind the iconostasis, the sacred screen that carried the icons of Christ and the apostles. In small communities, the priest and the deacon would function alone. That means, for long periods these two would perform rituals and prayers together, in a somewhat intimate closeness, invisible to the congregation. It is not difficult to see that this would inevitably lead to suspicions of impropriety if the deacon were a woman. This is precisely the kind of scandal the Council of Nicea (AD 325) wanted to prevent:

We decree that bishops shall not live with women; nor shall a priest who is a widower; neither shall they escort women; nor be familiar with them, nor gaze upon them persistently. And the same decree is made with regard to every celibate priest, and the same concerning such deacons as have no wives. And this is to be the case whether the woman be beautiful or ugly, whether a young girl or beyond the age of puberty, whether great in birth, or an orphan taken out of charity under pretext of bringing her up. For with such tools the devil slays religious, bishops, priests, and deacons, and incites them to the fires of desire.[12]

It simply was not pastorally prudent for a woman deacon to assist the bishop in this particular role. But did that mean she was not allowed to approach the altar?

God's "holy table"

We are familiar with the Western hysteria of keeping women away from the altar. Latin Fathers and local church synods increasingly excluded women from access to the altar. This culminated in medieval church lawyers decreeing that no woman, not even a consecrated nun, should "touch the sacred vessels or altar cloths," "carry incense around the altar," "handle consecrated vessels," or "wear sacred vestments."[13] Martimort seems to think that this applied to women deacons in the Byzantine communities, but did it?

Take the example of the candidates' posture at ordination. Martimort confidently asserts that the male ordinand genuflected on one knee, but the woman ordinand "was not allowed to genuflect." The man rested his head on the altar, the woman did not: "she received no power pertaining to the altar and, indeed, did not even have access to the altar."

How do we know the male candidate rested his head against the altar? It is present-day practice. It is not mentioned in the ordination rites. Now it may well be an old custom *presupposed* in the rites. But then we may equally presuppose that when the woman bowed, she too rested her head against the altar. If there had been a difference and it was significant, this would surely have been expressly stated in the rituals.[14]

Why then did the woman *bow* instead of genuflect? Liturgists provide a simple explanation: because of propriety. "Kneeling was considered an improper posture for a woman."[15] This is confirmed by the Chaldean ordination rite of women deacons which states, "The archdeacon presents the deaconess-candidate to the bishop; her hands are joined, and her head is bowed; she bows deeply from the waist, not, however, bending the knee, which would be improper."[16]

And as to access to the altar, the ordination rite goes out of its way to show that women deacons are *not* denied access, even though serving at the eucharist would not be their specific task:

- The ordination of the woman deacon took place in the sanctuary, near the altar. This is of great significance. Only bishops, priests, and deacons were ordained in the sanctuary; minor ministries were given at the Church entrance or in the sacristy. Theodore of Mopsuestia (350–429) explains the reason: "The law does not permit them [readers and subdeacons] to receive ordination in front of the altar because they do not minister at this mystery [i.e., at the sacred service of the altar]."[17] In other words: only those who serve at the altar are ordained at the altar.[18]

- At communion, the woman deacon receives communion in the sanctuary behind the closed screen and directly from the bishop, as the male deacons do: first a piece of the host on her hand, then a drink from the chalice which the bishop is still holding, as he does for all priests and deacons.

- What happens afterward is even more telling. The ritual prescribes, "When the newly ordained [woman] has taken part of the sacred body and precious blood, the archbishop hands her the chalice. She accepts it and puts it on the holy table [i.e., the altar]." This means that *after receiving communion herself,* she is handed the chalice which she holds and then puts on the altar herself. She does not distribute communion in church, as the newly ordained male deacon does — for reasons explained above. But she is, in principle, empowered to distribute communion. It amounts to what theologians call a degree of *potestas in eucharistiam,* authority regarding the eucharist.[19] Women deacons took communion to the sick.[20]

An analysis of the ordination rite shows, therefore, that the woman deacon was given access to the altar. She received, in principle, the same diaconal powers as the male deacon, even though her immediate tasks partly differed. Her tasks mainly consisted in assistance at the baptism of adult women and the material and spiritual care of sick women. These tasks were liturgically so important that they required the sacramental service of fully ordained women deacons. We will discuss this in the next chapters.

8

Just a minor role at baptism?

ALL THE EVIDENCE from ancient sources points at women deacons having played an indispensable role during the baptism
of women. Martimort denies this. I quote some typical derogatory
remarks:

> The part of deaconesses in baptism was very restricted. They
> simply completed the anointing begun by the celebrant.[1]

> If neither St. John Chrysostom, nor Theodore of Mopsuestia,
> nor the Antochian rituals, nor the Jerusalem Catechism made
> any mention of deaconesses in the celebration of baptism, this
> silence seems to indicate that, in the particular churches repre-
> sented by these writers, there was no perceived need to confer
> any such ministry upon deaconesses.[2]

> There are only two indications in the literature suggesting that
> deaconesses in Constantinople ever had anything to do with
> baptism.[3]

Silence in some sources proves nothing. The practice could be so
self-evident that there was no need to mention women deacons explicitly.[4] Moreover, Theodore of Mopsuestia says that the anointing
at baptism is done by those "who are designated for this ministry."[5]
John Chrysostom says in one place that the bishop "begins," "ar-
ranges for" the anointing, which again implies help.[6] Again, all the
authors mentioned have women deacons in their dioceses and express regard for their ministry. Specifically, and also applying directly
to Constantinople, the legislation of Justinian (535) describes the task
of the woman deacon as "ministering to the revered rites of baptism

and to be part of other hidden rites, which they rightly perform in connection with the venerable mysteries."[7]

The woman deacon played a crucial role in the baptism of women. She helped instruct the catechumens, she disrobed the women, anointed them over their whole bodies, descended with them into the baptismal font, dried them and dressed them in their baptismal robe. This is something a man could not do in Greek Byzantine culture, except in exceptional circumstances such as emergency baptisms when the rites were truncated.

The *Didascalia* of the Apostles gives this instruction to bishops:

> When women go down into the water [of the baptismal font], it is necessary that those going down into the water be anointed with the oil of anointing by a woman deacon. Where no other woman is present, especially where no woman deacon is at hand, it will then be necessary that the man who is performing the baptism anoints the woman being baptized [himself], but then he should only put his hand on their heads when anointing them. But where another woman is present, especially a woman deacon, it is not good for women to be seen by a man.... Afterward, whether you yourself are carrying out the baptisms, or whether you have entrusted that responsibility to the deacons and priests, a woman deacon should anoint the women, as we have already indicated.[8]

"It is not good for women to be seen [naked] by a man." This principle is repeated in Epiphanius of Salamis in Cyprus (315–403), the *Apostolic Constitutions,* and many other writings. This made women deacons indispensable, as we will see when we look at the details and the significance of the full baptismal ritual.

The gateway of baptism

In our low-key, matter-of-fact Catholic observance we have lost the awe which the early Christians felt for baptism. For them it was the entrance into a whole new way of life, radiant as the Risen Lord.

St. Cyril of Jerusalem sings its praise in many sermons. He calls baptism a "ransom to captives," a "forgiveness of offenses," the "death of sin," the "regeneration of the soul," "the garment of light," the "holy and indissoluble seal," the "chariot to heaven," the "luxury of paradise," an "entrance into the kingdom," the "gift of adoption." Catechumens became "Christians" and "faithful" only after the initiation of baptism. Only then could they take part in the central mysteries of the eucharist.

The rite of baptism in the early Byzantine period can be reconstructed with some detail, although there will have been local variations. I will here present one typical description of the elaborate ritual, without justifying every single detail with laborious references. I refer to the established liturgical studies.[9]

When people expressed interest in becoming Christian, the local bishop or priest would test their sincerity and provide general information about the requirements for joining the Church. Serious candidates would then be admitted into the group of catechumens through an initial rite. They would be marked by the sign of the cross on the forehead, receive salt on the tongue, be blessed by an imposition of hands and be prayed over in an exorcism. A program of general introduction to Christian faith would be started, with the stress on Christian living, rather than doctrine. The more intense preparation for baptism would start only at the beginning of Lent.

Then catechumens were expected to fast, like other Christians. This involved not only abstaining from meat and wine, but also from sex and from attending the public baths, the games, the theater, and the races. They would come to church every day, were "exorcised" by the priest through a prayer, and would then listen to instructions by the bishop or a priest delegated by him. In the case of women this instruction was often supplemented by women deacons, who "taught unskilled and rural women with clear and sound words, both as to how to respond to the questions put by the celebrant at the moment of baptism and how to live after the reception of baptism."[10]

About two weeks before Easter, the catechumens would be required definitely to subscribe their names for baptism. They would need to be recommended by someone who was already a Christian, who so became their sponsor. At about the same time the bishop would, for the first time, reveal the "creed" which would be explained line by line in the subsequent week. The catechumens would learn the creed by heart so that they could be examined on its contents at the beginning of Holy Week.

On Maundy Thursday they would break the fast and take a bath. They would attend some of the ceremonies of Good Friday and then present themselves for baptism on Holy Saturday, the vigil before Easter.

Dying and rising with Christ

After the readings of the vigil, the bishop would preach. This was followed by a ceremony of renunciation in which all the catechumens shared. If the baptistry was too small, the bishop, priests, deacons, and catechumens might walk to a side aisle near the baptistry. The catechumens would take off their outer garments. Wearing just a long shirt, their tunic, they would be made to stand on sackcloth, the symbol of Adam and Eve's garments of sin. They would trample on it. Then they would be made to face west, the direction of sunset and death. They would now be asked the questions "Do you renounce Satan?" "Do you renounce his vanity?" and so on, to each of which they would reply, "I do." In some churches this was followed by a hissing, to ridicule and curse the devil. It ended with a final prayer of exorcism.

The catechumens would now turn toward the east, the direction of the rising sun and of Christ's resurrection. In this position they would recite the Creed, or express their faith by responding "I believe" to questions such as "Do you believe in God, the Father?" "Do you believe in God the Son?" and so on.

Leaving the catechumens outside, the bishop would now enter the baptistry and bless the water in the font. He would also bless the jar containing the oil of catechumens (see the illustration on the following page). Baptism proper would now commence. First the men were

called in one by one and ministered to by the bishop and the deacon. When all the men had been anointed and baptized, the bishop and the male deacon would come out of the baptistry. It was now the turn of the women.

The officiating bishop would take up a position at the entrance to the baptistry. He would anoint the first female catechumen with a sign of the cross on her forehead, saying a prayer such as "Be anointed, [*name*], with the oil of gladness which overcomes all violence of the enemy and by which you will be protected in the name of the Father, the Son, and the Holy Spirit." Then the woman deacon would take her into the baptistry itself. There she would strip the catechumen of all her clothes and ornaments. She would untie the woman's hair "to ensure that nothing partaking of an alien spirit should descend with her into the water of second birth."[11] The woman deacon would pour some oil from the jar into a small vial which she could hold in her left hand. Pouring some oil on her right hand, she would anoint the naked catechumen over every part of her body.

Ancient rubrics leave no doubt about both the stripping and the anointing being total:

The person to be baptized is stripped naked.... All silver and gold ornaments, and clothes, are taken off.... Anoint that person on breast, arms, stomach, back, in the middle of both hands, etc.

The deacon removes from the catechumen all clothes, ornaments, earrings and whatever they wear.... He pours the oil for anointing into the cup of his hand and rubs it on the whole body of the catechumen, also in between the fingers of his hands and the toes of his feet, and his limbs, and his front and his back....

Anoint every limb from the hairs on the skull down to the toes.[12]

Since the anointing was itself an exorcism, implying a healing from all evil related to the body, it is obvious that the genital areas could not be omitted. Moreover, the massaging of the aromatic oil on the skin of body and limbs, culminating in the rubbing of the oil on the scalp and the hair, was a deeply satisfying sensual experience, a feeling of being totally vulnerable and yet wonderfully wanted. It evoked emotions of utter cleansing, of being wholly accepted body and soul, of being molded for rebirth in a new life. The anointing of a woman in this intimate way demanded the service of another woman. Moreover, since it was such a key ceremony within holy baptism itself, it required with preference the service of a woman *minister* who had been ordained for this function:

Ordain a woman deacon who is faithful and holy for the ministrations toward women. For sometimes he [the bishop] cannot employ a deacon, who is a man, to serve the women, on account of unbelievers. You must therefore employ a woman deacon on account of the imaginations of the bad. For we stand in need of a woman deacon for many necessities; and most of all in the baptism of women. The [male celebrant] shall anoint only their forehead with the holy oil, and after him the woman deacon shall anoint them: for there is no necessity that the women should be seen by men.[13]

From the ancient rituals we can more or less reconstruct what happened next. Ancient baptistries were like small ponds, with steps leading into the water. The woman deacon led the (female) catechumen down the steps, from the west to the east, so that the catechumen faced east. In the middle the font was about waist deep. The woman deacon would also descend into the font. For men, this was a function which the main baptizer, the bishop or the priest, would do himself, namely, to immerse the catechumen three times, using a Trinitarian formula. How was this done in the case of women when the main celebrant, who was a man, could not stand so close to the naked catechumen?

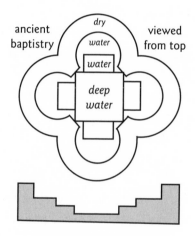

Cutaway viewed from the side

For women the immersion was done by the woman deacon while the baptismal formula was usually spoken by the bishop or priest who stood outside the baptistry, or perhaps behind a curtain inside the baptistry:

The deaconess [puts her hand on the head] of the woman to be baptized and plunges her three times into the water. The priest, meanwhile, invokes over her the three adorable names.[14]

A man [the male celebrant] should recite the invocation [ἐπικλη-σιν] over them in the water.[15]

It is conceivable that, in some places, the anointed catechumen was covered in a large veil and so led into the baptismal font, where the priest himself immersed her.[16] But this was not the usual practice. Baptism signified cleansing, washing, a getting rid of the excess oil that had now absorbed all the evil. This symbolism would be lost. The catechumen was immersed naked. The requirement that no man should see the female catechumen naked and that the conferring of baptism be done "with becoming decency" implied that the woman deacon rather than the bishop or priest performed the immersion. It is interesting that the Syriac tradition, which speaks about the veil, emphatically states that the woman deacon herself "performs both the anointing and the baptism."[17]

Imagine the physical excitement of the sign applied to the catechumen. Though mentally prepared, she would still feel the shock of chest and face being plunged into the cool water, head and hair totally submerged, then coming up gasping for breath and dripping. And this happened three times. Immersed in God! Frightening like being enclosed in a tomb, and yet strangely thrilling and invigorating. Here was a sacrament whose symbolism was imprinted on the memory.

Meanwhile the priest, from a distance, spoke the invocation, with words such as "This handmaid of God, [*name*], is baptized in the name of the Father [*first immersion*] — and of the Son [*second immersion*] — and of the Holy Spirit [*third immersion*]."

The woman deacon would now help the newly baptized woman step out of the font, walking toward the east. There she would "receive her," in the words of the ancient texts.[18] This meant dry her with a towel. Again, we should appreciate the exhilarating experience for the newly baptized. The woman deacon would gently rub her limbs dry, seeing to it that the oil that had soaked into the skin would still cling to it, making the neophyte feel healthy and whole and new all over. She would dry and comb her hair, thus completing a spiritual grooming that sealed the new Christian's admission into the community of faith.

The woman deacon would now dress her in a white robe, saying, "The handmaid of God [*name*] is clothed with the garment of righteousness, in the name of the Father, the Son, and the Holy Spirit," and conduct her to the bishop. The bishop would put the sign of the cross on her forehead with holy chrism, a special oil mixed with herbs and blessed for the purpose. Meanwhile he would say, "The seal of the gift of the Holy Spirit!"[19]

At the completion of the baptismal ceremonies, the newly baptized were welcomed by the other members of the Christian community:

> When the neophytes emerge from the sacred waters, all the congregation embraces them, greets them, gives them the kiss, congratulates them, and shares their joy. For once they were slaves and captives, now they have in an instant become free persons, children invited to the royal table. As soon as they ascend from the waters, they are led to the awesome table, the source of a thousand favors [i.e., the altar], they taste the body and the blood of the Lord and become the dwelling of the Spirit: they are clothed with Christ himself and, as such, everywhere they go, they appear, like terrestrial angels, as radiant as a burst of sunlight.[20]

Conclusion

It is clear from this sketch how important the role was which women deacons played during the baptismal liturgy. The female deacon was not the main celebrant but, like her male counterpart, assisted the bishop or priest in administering this crucial sacrament. She was associated with the most sacred moments of baptism, the anointing and the immersions. It is understandable that the Church ordained ministers who had been sacramentally dedicated to this task. It was a task that required trust. This is exactly what the ordaining bishop stated in the ordination prayers:

> You grant not only to men, but also to women the grace and coming of the Holy Spirit. Please, Lord, look on this your maidservant and dedicate her to the task of your diaconate, and pour

out into her the rich and abundant giving of your Holy Spirit.
Preserve her so that she may always perform her ministry with
orthodox faith and irreproachable conduct.

In an ordination prayer used in Georgia, the bishop invokes the
Spirit on the woman candidate with these words:

Promote this your handmaid to the ministry, that she may anoint
with oil the women that come to your holy baptism and bring
them to your holy font, so that she may become a deacon of
your church, according to the order of Phoebe whom the apostle
[Paul] ordained as minister in Cenchreae.[21]

9

No anointing of the sick?

T HE PASTORAL CARE of the sick featured strongly in the early Church. Here again anointing played a role. In Jesus' time, the disciples had "anointed many sick people with oil and cured them" (Mark 6:13). And the Apostle James had left this instruction:

> If one of you is ill, he should send for the elders [πρεσβυτερους] of the church. They must anoint him with oil in the name of the Lord and pray over him. The prayer of faith will save the sick person and the Lord will raise him up again. And if he has committed any sins, he will be forgiven. (James 5:14–15)

Women deacons were entrusted with the care of sick women. Did that include administering the sacraments to them? Martimort thinks not: "Only by means of errors in the interpretation of ancient texts has it been possible to imagine that deaconesses ever fulfilled a role in carrying out the sacramental anointing of the sick."[1]

Before we allow the evidence to speak for itself, a short introduction to the ancient liturgical practice seems appropriate. What did the anointing of the sick mean to Christians, and how was it done?[2]

Healing for body and soul

People in the Middle East used oil, mixed with herbs, as one of their most potent medicines. Applying not just natural but "sacred" oil added the bonus of spiritual power. Moreover, confession, as we know it today, was extremely rare. Christians received priestly absolution from their sins only once during their lifetime. Being anointed in their final illness was a critical last chance they had of receiving forgiveness for any sins that might remain. Such a rite of spiritual cleansing by sacred oil also opened the way to receiving holy communion on one's death bed, the viaticum that guaranteed a passage to eternal life. The final rites of preparing a Christian for death belonged to the *disciplina arcana,* the secret discipline that was known only to initiates, just like the central part of the eucharist from which catechumens were excluded. The Syrian mystic Aphraates (fourth century) speaks of the holy oil that "anoints the sick and by its secret mystery restores penitents."[3]

When priests were called to a sick person, they would often consecrate new holy oil in the home of the Christian family itself. Prayers for blessing the oil have been preserved in a number of ancient documents. God was asked to bestow supernatural efficacy upon the oil "for grace and remission of sins, for a medicine of life and salvation, for health and soundness of soul, body, and spirit." If the person had not confessed his sins before, this might now be done before the anointing.

The anointing itself was applied to the whole body, with special attention paid to the parts that caused pain or distress.[4] Its purpose was to purify all the limbs from the sin that might still adhere to them. The anointing of each member was accompanied by a specific prayer. Anointing the eyelids, the priest would say something like "Through this holy unction and his most tender mercy may the Lord pardon you whatever sins you have committed through sight." For the feet, "sins committed by walking." For the hands, "sins committed by touch"; and so on. While the loins were anointed, the priest prayed, "sins committed through carnal pleasure."

There also existed general prayers, such as this one preserved in Byzantine rituals:

> Holy Father, physician of souls and of bodies, you sent your Only-Begotten Son as the healer of every disease and our savior from death. Heal also your servant/handmaid [*name*] from the bodily infirmity that holds him/her, and make him/her live through the grace of Christ, by the intercessions of Saints [*patron saints*] and all the saints.[5]

When the anointing had been completed the sick person would be given holy communion.

It would seem that, whenever possible, priests were called in to perform these rites. And in the West, since the Councils of Florence and of Trent, it has become a matter of Church discipline that only the priest is the "proper" minister of the sacrament.[6] But the early practice was more flexible, especially in the Christian East.

Once the oil for the sick had been blessed, it could on occasion be used by *any* Christian, just as any Christian could baptize in an emergency. Pope Innocent I declared in 416, "This [injunction of the Apostle James] must, without any doubt, be accepted and understood as applying to the faithful who are sick. They can be anointed with the holy oil of chrism. *Provided this oil has been made [blessed] by a bishop,* it may be used not only by priests, but by all Christians when they need to anoint themselves or others."[7] The pope clearly speaks in the context of the sacrament. His words are repeated by Caesarius of Arles, St. Bede, Amalarius of Metz, and others. There is no justification in saying that such a use of the sacred oil by ordinary Christians was not equivalent to the full "sacrament" administered by a priest.[8] Then what about women deacons?

Women deacons as ministers of anointing

One of the principal tasks of women deacons was caring for sick women. By no stretch of the imagination can this be reduced to a mere caring for their physical and medical needs. How could these deacons overlook the spiritual anguish of their patients, knowing the wonderful comfort that only the religious anointing could provide? Their diaconate was also, and primarily, a spiritual ministry, and this necessarily required the "sacrament" of the anointing. Historical facts confirm this.

Epiphanius, bishop of Salamis on Cyprus (315–403), considered the role of a woman deacon at the rites of the sick as being parallel to her role at baptism:

[The diaconate of women] is to preserve decency for the female sex, whether in connection with baptism [λουτρου] or in
connection with the examination of [women undergoing] suffering or pain, or whenever the bodies of women are required
to be uncovered, so that they need not be seen by men officiating ['ιερουργουντων], but only by the deaconess [διακονουσης],
who is authorized by the priest to minister to the woman at the
time of her nudity.[9]

The woman deacon assisted the priest, just as she did at baptism.
She was authorized by him to minister to the woman "at the time of
her nudity." This could be an examination of the body and an anointing, while the priest stood nearby, perhaps in an adjoining room. But,
more likely, as we will see presently, she could have been sent to the
home. And, of course, when she anointed the sick person, she would
use oil blessed by the priest for this purpose.

A similar conclusion can be drawn from Justinian legislation in 535
that extols the ministry of women deacons, because they "approach
the sacred mysteries and minister to the revered rites of baptism and
are part of other secret rites, which they rightly perform in connection
with the venerable mysteries."[10] The "secret rites," mentioned again
in parallel with baptism, can be none other than those administered
to the sick and the dying.

At times the priest and the woman deacon will have performed
the sacred rites together. But this was not always possible. Often
the woman deacon had to perform the rites on her own. This is
what the *Didascalia* and the *Apostolic Constitutions* state in so many
words:

You [bishop] need the ministry of women deacons for many
reasons. The fact is that women deacons are necessary for
those houses of pagans where Christian women are also living. Women deacons can go there and visit those who are ill,
serve them in all their needs, and, again, bathe those who are
beginning to recover from their illness.[11]

Ordain also a woman deacon who is faithful and holy, for the ministrations toward women. For sometimes you cannot send a deacon, who is a man, to the women, on account of unbelievers. You shall therefore send a woman who is a deacon, on account of the imaginations of the bad.[12]

Just as in the case of the nakedness of women — which no man should see — so here we have another cultural problem. Men could not visit the inner rooms reserved to women. Already Clement of Alexandria (150–215) had indicated this as a major reason for involving women in the ministry. "The Apostles took women with them, not as wives, but as sisters, that they might be their co-ministers [συνδιακονους] in dealing with women in their homes. It was through them that the Lord's teaching penetrated also the women's quarters without any scandal being aroused."[13] This applied especially to the Greeks, as the Roman historian Cornelius Nepos recorded:

What Roman would blush to take his wife to a dinner-party? What Roman matron does not frequent the front rooms of her dwelling and show herself in public? But it is very different in Greece; for there a woman is not admitted to a dinner-party, unless no one is present except relatives. She keeps to the more retired part of the house called the "women's apartment," to which no man has access who is not next of kin.[14]

Christian women who were lying sick at home, perhaps even on their deathbed, could not be visited by any of the male ministers, especially if non-Christians too lived in the home or if non-Christians were close neighbors. This must often have been the case if we remember the crowded living conditions of Hellenist towns. The woman deacon had to serve these sick women in *all* their needs, we are told. How could this exclude what the patient would need most as a believer: the sacred anointing and partaking of holy communion? An ancient pastoral principle existed in the Church that "no sick person should depart from this world without holy communion."[15] Was this not precisely one of the reasons why women deacons were sacramentally ordained?

Other sources have left traces of this sacramental ministry of women. The "Canons of the Holy Apostles" (c. 320) describe the ministry [διακονια] for women as "a ministry of comfort for those who are in need."[16] This must include *Christian* comfort, the spiritual comfort for those who suffer and die only available in Christ (2 Corinthians 1:3–7). Women deacons took communion to the sick, according to the "Testament of the Lord" (c. 450).[17] Giving communion to women and anointing the sick are tasks of women deacons recorded in Syriac and Maronite sources.[18] St. Gregory of Nyssa (335–94) praised his sister St. Macrina, who ministered to sick and dying women, saying that: "she anointed her own hands through her mystical services."[19]

Some women deacons ministered in nursing homes for the sick and the dying. A tombstone from Jerusalem of the fifth century (see illustration) honors the deacon Eneon, who ministered to the sick: "+Tomb of Eneon, daughter of Neoiketis, deaconess of this hospital."[20] It is natural that her care would extend to the spiritual welfare of her patients.

It is interesting to note that *after* the anointing of the sick, there was another function, namely, that of "washing" the sick person when she got better. Ancient rubrics concerning the anointing of the sick warn the anointed person "not to remove the oil for seven days, just as the neophytes do." The oil was then washed off in a special bath.[21] This explains a phrase in the *Didascalia*, shown below in italics, which I have not seen commented on in any publication.

> You need the ministry of women deacons for many reasons. The fact is that women deacons are necessary for those houses of pagans where Christian women are also living. Women deacons can go there and visit those who are ill, serve them in all their needs and, again, *bathe those who are beginning to recover from their illness.*[22]

This bath too, which followed on the anointing of the sick, was another function that could not be done for a sick woman by a man, as the text implies.

Women deacons also assisted at washing and dressing the bodies of women who had died, for their burial. It is possible that the anointing of the sick was already seen, in case the person were to die, as a remote preparation for their Christian funeral. Elizabeth Carroll has rightly focused attention on women's role in the Gospels as ministers of anointing (Luke 7:46; John 11:2; 12:1–3). This reached its climax when Mary of Bethany anointed Jesus' body "in anticipation of his burial" (Mark 14:8; Matthew 26:12).[23]

Conclusion

Though many scholars leave this question as being undecided, I believe that we have sufficient evidence to assert that women deacons also assisted in the anointing of the sick.[24]

Scholars who specialize in the theology of the sacraments speak of the "matter" and the "form" of each sacrament, as we discussed in chapter 6. The matter is again comprised in the "remote matter" (such as water in baptism) and the "proximate matter" (immersion in the case of baptism). The remote matter for the anointing of the sick is the oil. The proximate matter is the act of anointing itself. In technical language, women deacons were personally and directly involved in the administering of both baptism and the sacrament of the sick by performing the "proximate matter": the immersions and the anointing. Though these actions *could* be performed by any Christian in case of necessity, women deacons were especially ordained to serve women in these central Christian rites.

10

Merely nuns, and not true deacons?

MARTIMORT MAINTAINS that the women deacons were not given the true diaconate, as received by men. They were only nuns, rewarded with an honorary blessing. He sees this reflected in the ordination prayers themselves, which, he contends, express dedication to a state of religious perfection: "Women who were accepted by God 'into the ranks of his ministers' consecrated themselves to *him* to serve in *his* 'holy places with a fitting holy desire.' They 'wished to consecrate' themselves to the Lord."[1] God's holy temple is the woman deacon's convent. "The deaconess was to 'persevere without reproach in God's holy temples'; she was to 'apply herself to household government,' which was the proper work precisely of the *hegumenē* [superior] of a convent of contemplative nuns but implied no other outside work or service; certainly it implied no liturgical role."[2]

Martimort notes that many of the women deacons recorded in history, like St. Olympias mentioned in chapter 1, were actually superiors of religious convents. And he closes with this parting shot:

> The patriarch Severus of Antioch found it appropriate to write that "in the case of deaconesses ... ordination is performed less with regard to the needs of the mysteries than exclusively with regard to doing honor." ... This honor was conferred on different categories of women: the wife of a priest or deacon; a widow of distinction; the *hegumenē* or superior of a convent.[3]

An objective look at the facts reveals a totally different picture.

Doing justice to a historical record

Let us start with Severus of Antioch. He was a Monophysite who became patriarch of Antioch for some years (512–57), after the Catholic bishop had been deposed.[4] Severus was condemned as a heretic by the Second Council of Constantinople (633). This does not necessarily disqualify him as a witness to existing Church practice, but we should read his words with circumspection. In the letter quoted by Martimort, Severus writes from exile in Egypt. This is the full text:

> In the case of women deacons, especially in convents, ordination is performed less with regard to the needs of the mysteries than exclusively with regard to doing honor. In the cities, however, women deacons habitually exercise a ministry relating to the divine bath of regeneration for the sake of women who are being baptized.[5]

Severus says just the opposite of what Martimort alleges. Yes, *sometimes* the diaconate is bestowed upon nuns as an honor, but even here their involvement in the mysteries is not ruled out. As to the women deacons attached to parish churches, they have a regular function in administering the sacrament of baptism, and obviously the other "mysteries," such as the anointing of the sick. And this, Severus wants to say, is precisely the reason why women are ordained, and should be ordained, in normal circumstances.

The link with convents

We need not be surprised at the fact that quite a few women deacons, also those working in a city apostolate, were nuns. For such a delicate and sacred ministry, women who had already dedicated themselves to a life of perfection would be the natural choice. When in the future women will be ordained deacons and priests in the Catholic Church, for example, we can be sure that religious sisters will be among them.

Moreover, for all members of the clergy, attachment to a church for the ministry and a residence without scandal were matters of great concern. The Council of Chalcedon (451) had forbidden any kind of "absolute ordination." Women deacons, like other clergy, had to be ordained *for a specific church*. A decree by Emperor Justinian in 535 fixed the number of women deacons attached to the Hagia Sophia as forty in number.[6] This number remained in force until 641. Like other clergy, the women deacons attached to a church were supported financially by that church "because of their ecclesiastical services."[7]

As in the case of bishops, priests, and male deacons, the Church feared sexual disgrace. Another decree of Justinian, also from 535, laid down the precaution that a woman deacon must either live on her own or in a convent or in a house with relatives where she could not give rise to scandal. This fear of scandal was not occasioned by her "being a nun," but by the fact that women deacons "approach the sacred mysteries and minister to the revered rites of baptism and take part in other secret rites, which they rightly perform in connection with the venerable mysteries."[8] A woman deacon who had an affair with a man was punished with the death penalty and with confiscation of all her possessions, not for breaking a religious vow of chastity, but for "shaming her ordination [χειροτονιαν]" and betraying "her priestly ministry [τηι 'ιεροσυνηι]."[9]

The ordination prayers

Contrary to what Martimort insinuates, the ordination prayers do not dedicate a woman deacon to a life of religious perfection, but to the full diaconate. The "holy house" to whose service the woman deacon is dedicated is the church and its congregation, not a convent. The ministry she is ordained for is not to guide a community of nuns, but the well-known, established, classical diaconate. "Dedicate her to the task of your diaconate ['εργον της διακονιας σου], and pour out into her the rich and abundant giving of your Holy Spirit." This is exactly the same as in the ordination prayer for the male deacon which mentions Stephen, "whom you had called as the first to the work of your diaconate ['εργον της διακονιας σου]." The male deacon's prayer also calls it "the work of the deacon" ['εργον του διακονου]. "Preserve her so that she may always perform her ministry [λειτουργια] with orthodox faith," etc. For both the male and female ordinand the term ministry (λειτουργια) is frequently used, together with the accompanying words of the same root: "ministering," "minister" (λειτουργος), etc. There is no implication here that the woman deacon would be less than the male deacon. "Fulfil in her the grace of the diaconate (της διακονιας), as you have granted to Phoebe the grace of your diaconate (της διακονιας σου), whom you had called to the work of the ministry [λειτουργιας]."

As we know from the Fathers of the Church, both Stephen and Phoebe were venerated as exemplary deacons. The bishop prays that the same grace of the diaconate that was in these two models may be in the ordinand. Moreover, the Greek "fulfil" means more than just "*give* her the grace." It expresses a completeness that leaves nothing wanting in the imparting of the sacrament. The phrase is used only in ordination prayers for the "major" orders, not in appointment prayers for the "minor" orders.[10]

A fourth-century tombstone, again in Jerusalem (see the illustration above), commemorates a deacon called Sophia: "Here lies the servant and bride of Christ, Sophia, the (woman) deacon ['η διακονος], the second Phoebe, who fell asleep in peace on the 21st of the month of March during the 11th... God the Lord..."[11] The phrase "the second Phoebe" reflects the Hellenistic practice of paying tribute to a person by comparing him or her to a great ancestor or model: "a second Homer," "a second Thecla," "a second Hercules."[12] Sophia is honored as someone who completed the ministry of the diaconate as fully and faithfully as the legendary St. Phoebe who was believed to have been ordained by Paul himself.

Unless the ordaining bishops did not know what they were saying, they clearly expressed the reality that these women received the full diaconate, just like their male counterparts.

What about the diaconate stole?

The ordination ritual prescribes: "[The bishop] puts the stole of the diaconate [το διακονικον ὡραριον] around her neck, under her veil, arranging the two extremities of the stole toward the front." Martimort attributes great significance to the fact that the male deacon received the stole differently, i.e., sideways, over one shoulder. "The rubric demonstrates that the deaconess did not wear the orarion in the same way as did the deacon; it was not wrapped all the way around her neck, and the two ends were brought out in front."[13]

To understand what the rubric says, it will help to study a mosaic in the oratory of San Venanzio in Rome, dated 642. The mosaic was made under Popes John IV and Theodorus, both Greeks by birth. The image shows Mary praying with her hands outstretched. Her main dress is a tunic. Her veil, the *maphorion,* is part of the mantle. It covers her head and her upper body and flows down all the way to just above her ankles, revealing the tunic in front. Coming down from underneath her veil, but over the tunic, we can see a bishop's pallium marked with a cross. Women deacons wore their stole in the same way, but in their case two extremities would hang in front.

With the male deacon, the bishop removed the man's scarf and then lifted the stole over his head and around his right arm, so that it could hang down from the left shoulder. This the bishop obviously could not do with a woman, for reasons of propriety. It would also mean that the woman was unveiled in church, which went against

established practice. Since the symbolism prescribed that the bishop had to impose the stole, rather than that he hand it to the woman deacon to put on for herself, the proper thing for him to do was to lift the back of her veil from her shoulders, adjust the stole around her neck under the veil and pull the two extremities to the front. This is exactly what the rubric says he should do.

The diaconal stole [το διακονικον 'ωραριον] was recognized as the specific emblem of the diaconate. The Synod of Laodicea (363) strictly forbade subdeacons, readers, or singers to wear the diaconal stole.[14]

Conclusion

Some women deacons were nuns at the same time, often superiors of convents so that they could attend to the spiritual needs of their sisters. This may explain how in the West traces of the diaconate ordination were retained in the installation of prioresses and abbesses of some orders of women. But this custom does not reflect the original diaconate, neither in its sacramental status nor in the pastoral tasks of its ministry.

In twelfth-century Europe, a man became a knight only after trial and apprenticeship in war. Knighthood made him a professional cavalry warrior. His duties involved loyalty to the king and readiness to enforce royal wishes through police action or in military combat. The knightly ideal, sung in ballads, required honesty, respect for women, championing the cause of the poor. A knight's privileges consisted in being given land and tax relief. Does being "knighted" by the queen of England today convey the same status? Historical realities cannot be judged by their shadows.

Were the Byzantine women deacons true and full *deacons*? They obviously were. The Church recognized them as full deacons. It imparted the full diaconate ordination to them and gave them the distinctive diaconate stole to wear. Church Councils called them deacons. In civil legislation women deacons enjoyed the same privileges and were punished with the same sanctions as their male colleagues. The laws of Justinian more than once mention the men and women under one heading: "men and women deacons."[15] What further proof do we require?

11

Only a rare and local phenomenon?

T HROUGHOUT HIS BOOK, Martimort harps on the fact that the ministry of women deacons was a "limited phenomenon." He points out that the diaconate of women never struck deep roots in large sections of the Christian world. Women deacons did not flourish in Coptic Egypt and Ethiopia, he says, nor among the Latin-culture populations of North Africa, Gaul, Spain, Britain, northern Italy, and other European countries.

Now we have no quarrel with him here. Church Councils such as those of Chalcedon and Trullo may have given it a status in the universal Church by laying down conditions for it, but in actual fact it did not catch on in the West. Big deal. It flourished in the Byzantine countries which formed the heartland of the Church at the time.

Martimort counters that even in the Greek-speaking regions of the Church, the occurrence of women deacons was only sporadic. To illustrate this assertion, he points to the recorded anecdote of a monk called Conon. The event narrated is supposed to have happened in the sixth century.

Father Conon, who hailed from Cilicia (just north of Antioch), had joined the monastery of Penthucla in Palestine, not far from Jerusalem. The monastic chapel also served as a parish church for the local people. Conon had been appointed by the community to look after baptisms. Often this required "anointing and baptizing" adults, including women. It left Conon troubled about his chastity:

One day a young woman from Persia came to be baptized. She was so beautiful and so fair that the priest did not have the courage to anoint her with holy oil. Since she stayed there for two days, Archbishop Peter [of Jerusalem] heard about this. He was concerned and wanted to designate a woman deacon [διακονονγυναικα] for this function; but he did not do it, since the place did not permit it.

Conon fled to a deserted place and asked his patron, St. John the Baptist, to come to his aid. St. John urged him, in a vision, to overcome the temptation manfully. Conon said he could not. Eventually St. John relented and fortified him against temptation through a strange ceremony. He made Conon sit upon a rock, took off his clothes, and marked him three times with the sign of the cross "below his navel" (i.e., on his genital area) and assured him that he would now be equal to the struggle:

> Father Conon returned to the monastery where he used to baptize. The next morning he anointed and baptized the young woman from Persia without even knowing that she was a woman. He kept this office for twelve years, anointing and baptizing, without any movement of the flesh and without noticing any woman.[1]

Reflecting on the tale

I do not understand how this amusing story proves that women deacons were employed rarely. To begin with, it confirms one of the reasons why women deacons were ordained: to forestall the embarrassment of a male priest anointing the female catechumen all over her body. Surely, Father Conon's remedy is not recommended as a universal solution!

Moreover, the archbishop immediately thought of assigning a woman deacon. The difficulty was that it was not appropriate for a woman deacon to be employed in a monastery of men. This is what the phrase: "the place did not permit it" obviously means. Having a woman deacon attached to a church also implied providing for her income, as we see from Justinian legislation. All this may well show up a problem experienced by rural monasteries engaged in pastoral work; it does not disprove the general prevalence of women deacons.

In Cilicia, where Conon was born, five tombs honoring the memory of women deacons have been found: of Timothea, Athanasia, Theodora, Theophila, and Charitina.[2] In and around Jerusalem itself, near Conon's monastery, four women deacons are recorded on tombstones, including Eneon, mentioned in chapter 9, and Sophia, mentioned in chapter 10; outside Jerusalem, still in Palestine, another four: Maria, Elladis, Nonna, and Anasthasia.[3]

The evidence

In the course of the preceding chapters I have already had occasion to refer to the many literary documents that attest to the women's diaconate. The main records can be examined in the Texts section of this book.

The ancient calendar of saints for the Greek-Byzantine part of the Church fixed feast days for twenty-six women deacons. Some of their life stories have been preserved for us, even though these have often been colored by the piety of medieval biographers who preferred to present women deacons as precursors of the devout nuns of their time.[4] In spite of this, they provide evidence for the impact women deacons had upon their local church communities.

Seven women deacons (feast day: May 16) are remembered as having been martyred with Bishop Abdjesus in fifth-century Persia, with sixteen priests, nine male deacons, and six monks. St. Poplia (feast day: October 9) was venerated as a "confessor," because she had been tortured for her faith under Emperor Julian at Antioch in 362. St. Apollonia in Alexandria (feast: February 9) was beaten till she had lost all her teeth and then burnt alive by a jeering pagan crowd (third century).

St. Melania the Younger (feast: December 31) had been born in Rome (fourth century). She ended up living in Jerusalem, where she established a monastery on the Mount of Olives. She converted many pagans, including Gerontius, who later became a priest. St. Domnika

(feast: January 8) was ordained to the "priestly rank of the diaconate of Christ" by Patriarch Nektarios in Constantinople. She specialized in the ministry of the sick and became famous for her physical and spiritual healing.

Many women deacons worked alongside their brothers, husbands, and fathers in the apostolate. St. Theosebia (feast: January 10) was the wife of bishop St. Gregory of Nyssa. St. Gregory of Nazianzen's wife, St. Nonna (August 5), was a woman deacon, and so was his daughter, St. Gorgonia (February 23). The brothers St. Basil the Great and St. Gregory of Nyssa had a sister who is venerated as a woman deacon, St. Macrina (July 19).

It is obvious that these women were held in great esteem, and in devotional literature it is usually their piety and otherworldliness that are extolled. It is then easy to overlook that we are talking about real women who performed the day-to-day ministry of women expected of ordained women deacons.[5] We gain further insights from funeral inscriptions.

Here lies the deacon [ἡ διακονος] Maria of devout and happy memory who, in accordance with the word of the Apostle [prob. 1 Tim. 5:10], cared for children, welcomed strangers, washed the feet of the saints [i.e., the Christians], and shared her bread with the needy. Remember her, Lord, when she arrives in your Kingdom. (Archelais, Cappadocia, sixth century)[6]

Here lies the servant of the Lord, Theoprepia, a virgin all her life and deacon [διακ] of Christ, who has completed a self-disciplined, zealous, and exemplary life in the Lord God. (Bonitsa, Macedonia, fourth century)[7]

We the poor of Gargathis have plastered and renewed this sarcophagus to the memory of Eugenia the deacon [διακονου]. (Bithynia, fourth century?)[8]

At present, at least thirty-two distinct inscriptions concerning women deacons are known from the countries belonging to the Byzantine empire between 200 and 800 (see the map on page 97). They stand alongside tombstones dedicated to bishops, priests, and male deacons. Does this give us an idea of *how many* women deacons there have been? Only few tombs have survived the ravages of time, so we may safely estimate that the surviving ones represent fewer than one in every thousand tombs of prominent Christians of that era. And, of course, tombs with inscriptions were not erected for all women deacons. Thirty-two tombs of women deacons would then point to there having been a minimum of 32,000 women deacons during that period. This figure may not seem extravagant if we recall that forty women deacons ministered at Hagia Sophia Cathedral in Constantinople alone in 535.[9]

The global view

The ministry of women never got a foothold in the Latin-speaking countries because of Roman law, as I have documented elsewhere.[10] It is noteworthy all the same that in spite of the cultural and social restrictions laid on women by Roman culture the phenomenon of women's diaconate *did* occur there too. For example, in Gaul, we have the cases of women deacons such as St. Radegunde and St. Genevieve, the patron saint of Paris. It is also highly significant that a number of local Church synods in Gaul laid down that "women should *no longer* be ordained deacons."[11] This obviously points to an existing practice that was at least considered legitimate in the Western Church until that time. Also, it may have been discontinued for purely local reasons, for no judgment is made against its universal use in other parts of the wider Church.

To establish a Church practice we do not need to show that it was accepted by all local churches everywhere all the time. A legitimate practice well established in one section of the Church, such as the custom of not rebaptizing members of a Christian sect whose baptism was judged to be valid, was then accepted by the universal Church as a legitimate practice. Diverging marriage practices, observed in different sections of the Church for centuries, were later integrated into universal Church law. The personal and secret confession of sins was known only in some countries during the first millennium. The existence of this practice for a number of centuries in such countries was taken as proof of the fact that the practice was legitimate and could be extended to the wider Church.

Until the eighth or ninth century, the center of gravity of Christianity lay in the East. Western Europe had been overrun by the migrating nations from the Caucasus. The western part of the Roman Empire had collapsed. The Christian communities of North Africa were wiped out. The small Christian minorities in Gaul and Britain were struggling for survival in a political and social turmoil. The barbarians of northern Europe, such as the Saxons, the Friesians, the Angles, the Vikings, and others were being evangelized with varying success.

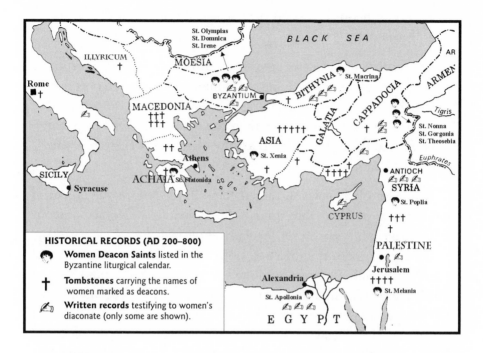

HISTORICAL RECORDS (AD 200–800)

🧑 **Women Deacon Saints** listed in the Byzantine liturgical calendar.

† **Tombstones** carrying the names of women marked as deacons.

✍ **Written records** testifying to women's diaconate (only some are shown).

Meanwhile the ancient Christian churches continued to flourish in the East, protected as they were by the imperial power now firmly entrenched in Constantinople. It is in these countries that women deacons were firmly established. The area included Asia Minor, Bithynia, Cappadocia, Cilicia (that is, present-day Turkey), Syria, Judea, Thrace, Macedonia, and Achaia (that is, present-day Greece), Sicily, and Cyprus.

From the ninth century onward the diaconate of women gradually declined also in the East for a number of reasons. Adult baptisms had become rare, since few converts joined the Christian communities. Priests had easier access to the homes of the sick, where the anointing of women was restricted to imposing oil on the forehead. Perhaps, fear of women's menstruation was an additional cause. Theodore Balsamon (1105–95), a church lawyer in Constantinople, wrote as follows:

> Formerly there were recognized orders of deaconesses, and they too had their place in the sanctuary. But the impurity of their

menstrual periods dictated their separation from the divine and holy sanctuary.[12]

Today deaconesses are no longer ordained although certain members of ascetical religious communities are erroneously styled deaconesses. For there is a law that prohibits women from entering the sanctuary. How then could a woman who does not even have the right to approach the altar, possibly exercise the office of deacon?[13]

Balsamon obviously contradicts himself. He reflects the historical ignorance of his time. But, though the ordination of women deacons fell into disuse, it was never formally abolished.[14]

For our purpose it suffices to note that in the Byzantine part of the Church, fully Catholic until the schism between East and West in 1054, the sacramental diaconate of women existed as an undeniable reality. It was enshrined in the official liturgical books of ordination. It was part of the official law of the Church as laid down at the universal Councils of Chalcedon (451) and Trullo (692). It was sanctioned by the imperial laws of the state (535).[15]

12

Did the bishops not *intend* to ordain real deacons?

IN CHAPTER 6 we discussed the fact that during the first millennium Christians did not yet use the term "sacrament" in the technical sense we use it in today. Yet the *reality* of sacrament existed in the Church at the time, and no theologian today would dispute that bishops, priests, and male deacons truly received holy orders and thus "the sacrament of holy orders" in today's terms. Then what about women deacons? Did they receive the sacrament? Since the rite to ordain women was essentially the same as that to ordain men, the answer is obviously "yes," as we saw in chapter 5.

What matters, of course, is whether the bishops at the time intended to impart a full ordination to women. Now there is no way we can establish that intention except by studying what the bishops said and did while performing the ordination. The fact that women were ordained through an "imposition of hands" [χειροτονια] was significant. However, it does not by itself prove the sacramental character of the ceremony, for during the first centuries this gesture was also employed for the imparting of minor orders.[1] To determine whether an ordination was a sacrament or not depends crucially on the *form* used, that is, what the bishops in their ordination prayers said they wanted to do, and the additional ceremonies which helped to define the precise nature of the *matter*, namely, whether hands were imposed for a full ordination. From this we can establish *the objective intention of the rite*.[2] True to form, Martimort raises objections, which we will now consider.

99

The setting of the ordination

It is significant that women deacons were ordained in the sanctuary, before the altar and right within the eucharistic celebration. This is how Martimort tries to minimize its significance:

> Vagaggini exaggerated the significance of the fact that the deaconess was ordained within the sanctuary, while subdeacons and lectors had to remain outside, either in the nave or in the *diaconicon* [the sacristy]. Certainly the distinction between the ordinations carried out inside the sanctuary and those carried out outside is a classic distinction.... Ordination at the altar was conferred only on those destined to serve at the altar. But the deaconess had no role at the altar, as all the ancient and medieval authors attested.... Thus it is not possible to find a theological reason for conducting the ordination of deaconesses in the Byzantine rite within the sanctuary.[3]

This is an incredibly twisted piece of reasoning. The place and point in time of the ordination, which are by Martimort's own admission significant, are dismissed as trivial because "the deaconess had no role at the altar"! We have already seen, in chapter 7, that women deacons *did* have access to the altar. But apart from that, should we not allow the liturgical symbolism to speak for itself? For its significance was not only to indicate access to the altar, but to mark the ordination as one of the "major orders," to distinguish it from other, supporting ministries such as the subdiaconate and the lectorate.

Theodore of Mopsuestia (350–429) explains the classic distinction. Notice how he defines the diaconate as a "ministry to sacred things," which certainly also included baptism:

> It is worth adding that we should not be surprised at the fact that he [Paul] does not mention subdeacons or lectors here. For these [functions] are actually outside the orders of real ministry in the Church. They were created later on by the need of many things that had to be done by others for the good of the mass of the

faithful. That is why the law does not permit them to receive ordination in front of the altar because they do not minister at this mystery. For the lectors look after the readings and the subdeacons in the sacristy prepare what is needed for the service of the deacons and look after the lights in church. However, only the priests and deacons perform the ministry of the mystery: the former by fulfilling their priestly role, the latter by ministering to sacred things.[4]

The Orthodox liturgist Simeon of Thessalonika confirms this in his classic work on ordination, written between 1418 and 1429: "Two ordinations are given outside the sanctuary, that of the reader and subdeacon. There are also others for administrators, deputees, acolytes.... But the exalted ordinations are imparted inside the sanctuary."[5]

The ordination of women deacons in the sanctuary "right in the heart of the Divine Liturgy" ranks it among the orders of the higher clergy (Evangelos Theodorou, Orthodox expert on women deacons).[6]

The public character of the ordination

Women deacons were ordained before the whole congregation and "in the presence of the priests, deacons, and deaconesses" (*Apostolic Constitutions*).[7] This is also clear from the standard Byzantine ordination rite, which mentions the other clergy.

This "public" character of the ceremony marks the ordination as one of the higher orders. A study of the procedure at ancient ordinations shows that the public election of the new minister belonged to the ordination itself. St. Jerome (347–419), for instance, records this in one of his letters:

In Alexandria, since Mark the Evangelist until Bishops Heraclas and Dionysius, the priests always instituted as their bishop one of their own, after having elected him and enthroned him; as soldiers do when they proclaim their emperor; or the deacons who elect one of their own as archdeacon because of his zeal.[8]

At times, as in this example, there seems to have been no imposition of hands. Normally, the imposition of hands with the invocation of the Spirit followed on the election. The point is that *the ecclesial context* of the ordination, expressed in the common election and public recognition by the congregation, was *crucial* at higher ordinations. Private ordinations, outside the congregation, were ipso facto invalid.[9] The public setting of the ordination of women deacons confirms its status as a major ordination.

The "Divine Grace" proclamation

We read this rubric in the ordination rite for women deacons: "The bishop says the 'Divine Grace' with a loud voice." This proclamation was only performed for the higher orders. Martimort refuses to recognize its significance in the case of women deacons. After saying that the proclamation was used for minor orders in the Melchite rite and occurs in a sixteenth-century *euchologion* to institute an archpriest and an abbot, he continues:

> Not a single existing manuscript contains the complete text of the Ἡ θεα χαρις for the ordination of deaconesses. Surely this text could not have been the same as was used at other ordinations, where the supposition always existed that the candidate already possessed the preceding degree of the ministry.[10]

The Melchite reference is irrelevant since we are discussing Byzantine practice. The one Byzantine ritual of later date Martimort refers to, which has another, later, and derived form of the Ἡ θεα χαρις, is not representative of the early tradition.[11]

We can be sure that the "Divine Grace" was the same in the case of women deacons and of male deacons, for a number of reasons. To begin with, the preceding degree of any ministry — contrary to what Martimort contends — was not essential, as ancient practice shows. Deacons did not need to be subdeacons first, before they could be ordained deacon. Second, the rubrics explicitly say that everything is the same for male or female deacons except where indicated. If the "Divine Grace" proclamation had been different for women, this would certainly have been mentioned.[12] Finally, the classic "Divine Grace" proclamation had a very rigid form with only three variable elements. This is the actual text:

> Divine Grace which always heals what is infirm and completes what is missing chooses so-and-so [*name*] as bishop [*or priest, deacon*] of [*name of the location*]. Let us therefore pray for him/her that the grace of the Holy Spirit may descend upon him/her.

Research has shown that this Byzantine form is very old indeed, going back to at least the third century. It was considered *the* distinctive characteristic of Christian ordination:

> The ordaining bishop speaks the proclamation with a loud voice. This mystery signifies that the ordainer, who is loved by God, is the herald of the divine choice. It is not he himself who leads the ordinand to ordination by his own grace, but he is moved by God in all ordinations. (Pseudo-Dionysius; c. 500)[13]

> [I never aspired to the priesthood], all the more because many of these ordinations happen through human ambition, not really by the divine grace. (St. John Chrysostom; 344–407)[14]

> [On the disorderly election of a bishop.] I would almost believe that political authorities are more ordained than ours over which one proclaims the "Divine Grace." (St. Gregory of Nazianzen; 330–89)[15]

The great liturgist Bernard Botte thought that the proclamation itself *was* the ordination, at least originally.[16] But later studies disproved this. Ordination consisted of two distinct stages of one and the same liturgical action, each equally essential: the *election* and the *ordination proper.* The election indicated who was chosen for the ministry. It proclaimed God's choice of candidate. It manifested the intention of the Holy Spirit. The imposition of hands was the

sacrament through which the Spirit actually descended on the ordinand.[17] The "Divine Grace" proclamation was therefore the public
act of election which designated a candidate to a particular ministry
in a specific church. In 398 Emperor Arcadius urged the bishops to
"grant the Divine Grace to John [Chrysostom] to ordain him bishop
of Constantinople."[18]

At ordinations, and particularly at Byzantine ordinations, the "Divine Grace" was proclaimed only for bishops, priests, and deacons.
The fact that the ordaining bishop proclaimed the "Divine Grace"
to announce the divine election of a woman deacon shows that
he ranked her ordination, without any shade of doubt, within the
sacrament of holy orders, like that of male deacons.

The calling down of the Spirit

The central action of ordination is the calling down of the Holy Spirit
on the ordinand:

> Do now look upon this your handmaid, who is to be ordained
> [προχειριζομενην] to the diaconate [εις διακονιαν], and grant
> her your Holy Spirit.[19]

> Dedicate her to the task of your diaconate [της διακονιας], and
> pour out into her the rich and abundant giving of your Holy
> Spirit.[20]

> Grant the gift of your Holy Spirit also to this your maid-servant
> who wants to dedicate herself to you, and fulfil in her the grace
> of the diaconate [διακονιας], as you have granted to Phoebe the
> grace of your diaconate [διακονιας].[21]

In the Eastern tradition, the calling down of the Holy Spirit is technically known as the *epiclesis*. During the divine liturgy, it is not so
much the "words of consecration" but the *epiclesis* that brings about
the transformation of the bread and the wine. *Epiclesis,* in one form
or other, occurs in all the sacraments, for the sacraments come about
through the action of the Spirit. Every *epiclesis* means a drawing on

the Spirit Christ obtained for us at Pentecost. The Church asks to receive from God here and now, what she has already historically received in Christ as a promise. This also applies to the ministries. The Pentecostal Spirit, "who provides all things," pours its fullness into the bishop, the priest, and the deacon.[22]

Being the action of the Spirit in the Church, the full *epiclesis* always takes place in the context of the assembled church community. The *epiclesis* of ordination also specifies the ministry for which the Spirit is imparted: as in the case of the woman deacon who receives the Spirit in view of the diaconate. Though indirect mention is made of the gifts of the Spirit in the installation prayers of some of the minor orders, it is only bishops, priests, and deacons on whom the full *epiclesis* is called down.[23]

The second ordination prayer

Having two ordination prayers is another indication that a major order is imparted. Martimort dismisses this feature as irrelevant for the woman deacon because the formulation of the second prayer is slightly different from that for the male deacon:

> For the ordination of a deaconess, as for the ordination of a [male] deacon, a priest, or a bishop, the officiating bishop pronounced two prayers, separated by a diaconal litany, and during each one he kept his hand on the head of the ordained. Is it necessary to point out, however, that the prayers pronounced in the case of the deaconess did not represent a simple transposition of those pronounced for a [male] deacon?[24]

I am stunned at this utter lack of perception on the part of someone who is supposed to be a liturgist. I have already shown, in chapter 10, that the ordination prayers clearly and explicitly designate women deacons to the diaconate. What I find hard to swallow is that Martimort refuses to admit the significance of having *two* prayers for women deacons, which is another sign of a full sacramental ordination.

The second ordination prayer, also known as the *ekphonese*, because the bishop spoke it softly, was a later development at the higher ordinations, probably starting from the fourth century. It may have been inspired by the need of the ordaining bishop to make sure that the conditions for ordination had been fulfilled. It may also manifest the typical Eastern trait of prayers spoken softly out of religious "awe and dread," as we encounter during the eucharist.[25]

By speaking the *ekphonese* prayer over the woman candidate, the bishop again indicated her being raised to the full sacrament of the diaconate.

As to the *contents* of the second ordination prayer, contrary to what Martimort says, both in the case of the man and the woman, the substance is the same. The man receives the Holy Spirit "for the ministry of the deacon," the woman "for the grace of the diaconate [διακονιας], as you have granted to Phoebe the grace of your diaconate [διακονιας], whom you had called to the work of the ministry [λειτουργιας]." Could the ordaining bishop be more outspoken? The woman is even more explicitly, forcefully, deliberately, and undeniably ordained to the diaconate than the man!

Conclusion

All the symbolism surrounding the imparting of ordination to the women signified its being a real sacrament:

+ its setting in the heart of the eucharist;

+ the presence of the clergy and the faithful;

+ the proclamation of divine election through the hallowed "Divine Grace" formula;

+ the *epiclesis* of the Holy Spirit on the ordinand;

+ the addition of the second, *ekphonese* prayer of ordination.

Through this symbolism the ordaining bishop indicated, both to the ordinand and to the assembled congregation, his unmistakable intention to impart a full, sacramental diaconate ordination to the woman.

If this was not a full sacrament, then neither was the ordination of bishops, priests, and male deacons.

13

Tackling the underlying assumptions

I N PREVIOUS CHAPTERS I have, quite a few times, expressed as-
tonishment at Martimort's apparent unwillingness to accept the
sacramental status of the women's diaconate in first millennium
Byzantium. I am not the only one to feel that way. Peter Hofrichter
of the University of Salzburg in Austria remarks, "Martimort's book
is an indispensable collection of material in connection with the issue
of deaconesses. But his arguments do not convince."[1] In 1987 Frederick McManus, the well-known American canonist and liturgist, made
the same observation when reviewing Martimort's book:

> One curious and fundamental flaw has to be noted. Almost with-
> out exception all the instances and all the functions attributed to
> deaconesses are evaluated negatively.... Instances, perhaps iso-
> lated or difficult to judge, whether of the presentation of the
> chalice to deaconesses or the use of "ordination" in relation to
> them, are uniformly and almost totally dismissed.... The reader
> might reach the very opposite conclusion: given the cultural and
> religious obstacles, the extraordinary thing is that any functions
> even slightly comparable to those of male deacons have been
> received in so many churches and at so many different times.[2]

It is natural to ask oneself, *Why* is Martimort so negative? What
is going on? McManus too senses some undeclared opposition: "Not
even in his rather negative conclusion [at the end of his book]
does Martimort state his thesis (or posture) explicitly, but his interpretations seem always to be in the negative."[3] What has been
suppressed?

In 1980 Martimort published a short article on "the question of women serving at the altar."[4] Basing himself on ancient sources, he came to the conclusion that women were never allowed access to the altar. Why? he asked himself. Rejecting two reasons indicated by the sources themselves, opposition to women priests in Gnostic sects (sixth century) and the fear of menstruation (mentioned by two Orthodox medieval theologians), he suggests that the only, unspoken ground underlying the tradition must be the intrinsic ordering of the diaconate to the priesthood, which is reserved to men alone.[5]

Suddenly, Martimort's book on deaconesses, which he wrote two years later, makes sense. Since diaconate, priesthood, and service at the altar are intrinsically linked in his view, the women's diaconate *cannot* have been a sacrament. For "at no time did deaconesses in the Byzantine rite ever have access to the sanctuary"; "the deaconess did not have access to the altar."[6] The cat is out of the bag. Here we have the hidden thesis, the undeclared posture McManus was looking for. Measured against the yardstick of this carefully disguised *systematic bias,* the findings about women deacons *had to be* negative.

When I speak of a "systematic bias," I am referring to a theological judgment that arises from an ideological position. It may cause a "blind spot" that filters out all contrary evidence. Everything is seen through the glasses of one's flawed *hermeneutics,* that is, the way one interprets data. This may affect even great scholars without their being aware of it.

When I worked in India in the 1960s and 1970s, I was instrumental in building up Christian literature for the Telugu-speaking people of Andhra Pradesh. I made a study of the ancient Telugu Christian classics which had been written by French missionaries from the seventeenth century onward. While I greatly admired the heroism, dedication, and scholarship of these pioneers of the faith, I was astonished at their blatant prejudice against local customs and Hindu religion in particular. Their writings overflowed with judgments that characterized Brahmins as "cheats" and "charlatans" and that dismissed everything Hindu as "idolatry" and "devil worship." The Hindu scriptures, which contain such moving records of profound spiritual search, were utterly rejected as "the arsenal of paganism we have to use to combat their errors."[7] I am sure that these French champions of Christianity were sincere, but their judgment was flawed, and we would be ashamed to publish their writings today.

Martimort's followers

Small wonder that Martimort is popular among those theologians in the Catholic Church who reject the ordination of women. And here the irony intensifies. We are presented with two pillars on which arguments against a sacramental diaconate of women are built up. *Theological pillar*: the diaconate stands totally in the service of the priesthood, which only men can receive; women cannot be ordained deacons, neither could they have been in the past. *Historical pillar*: women deacons were not sacramentally ordained, as Martimort has proved.

As one typical example, let us take Gerhard Ludwig Müller, professor at the University of Munich, who firmly opposes any thought of women being admitted to either the priesthood or the diaconate. Müller quotes St. Thomas Aquinas to prove that the diaconate, like the priesthood, is connected to the eucharist and therefore belongs to the one sacrament of holy orders. He then continues:

> With respect to the deaconess, Thomas summarizes the valid teaching of the Church. The male sex is a requirement for receiving the Order of the presbyterate and the diaconate . . . [Thomas says:] "Deaconess [in past documents] denotes a woman who shares in some act of the deacon, namely, who reads the homilies in church."[8]

Müller thus bases this theological judgment on writings by Thomas Aquinas, who, notwithstanding other achievements, had totally flawed views concerning women. Following Aristotle, Thomas believed that, without male genitals, women were not complete human beings.[9] The real force of generation resides in the male seed,[10] which derives energy from the heavenly bodies.[11] Men are also more intelligent than women,[12] which explains why women are subject to men.[13] Moreover, man is superior because he was created first,[14] and only man fully reflects God's image.[15] Small wonder that Thomas concluded that Christ had to be born as a male and only male priests can represent him, for "woman is in a state of subjection" and "the female sex cannot signify eminence of degree."[16] Hardly the kind of reasoning to build sound theology on today. Then what about Thomas's views on women's diaconate?

Aquinas obviously shared the ignorance of other medieval theologians about the real history of women deacons. But what *is* interesting — a point purposely passed over by Müller — is that if Thomas had *known* the true facts of women's diaconate, he might have changed his opinion on women in the ministries. For the full text reads:

> Some, however, have asserted that the male sex is necessary for the lawfulness and not for the validity of the sacrament, because even in the Decretals (cap. Mulieres dist. 32; cap. Diaconissam, 27, qu. i) mention is made of deaconesses and priestesses. But deaconess there denotes a woman who shares in some act of a deacon, namely, who reads the homilies in the Church; and priestess [*presbytera*] means a widow, for the word "presbyter" means elder.[17]

St. Thomas's historical ignorance is, perhaps, forgivable, but what about Müller's? Could he too be ignorant of the facts? Read this sweeping statement:

> In the oldest disciplinary Church text handed on in tradition [the *Traditio Apostolica*; AD 200] it is stressed that whereas the bishop, priest, and deacon receive the sacramental imposition of hands in view of their liturgical service, the reception of a woman into the order of widows is not performed through a sacramental ordination. In all the literary witnesses of the next centuries what stands out beyond any doubt is that it would be

impossible to appoint or ordain anyone to be a bishop, priest, or deacon, except a man.[18]

The *Traditio Apostolica* reflects the tradition of the Latin church in Rome. And indeed, it rejects the ordination of widows. So what? What about all the Greek evidence for ordained women deacons? How can Müller state that in all (!) the literary witnesses of the next centuries (!) it stands out (!) that it would be impossible (!) to ordain anyone to be a deacon except a man? Has he never heard about the ordination of women deacons, you wonder? Yes, he has. But he is cavalier when discussing their history.[19]

For instance, he rejects the validity of ancient records about women deacons, because "we encounter the title *diaconissa* as a designation for the wives of deacons."[20] This is a popular excuse, already found among medieval theologians, which refers to the usage of the term *diaconissa* in some Western, Latin sources.[21] This usage is never found in the Byzantine part of the Church where either "woman deacon" or "deaconess" always designates a deacon, ordained in her own right. It is obvious that Müller has not bothered to study the sources.

And about the ritual for ordaining women deacons, this is what he has to say:

> Although there are records of the liturgical installation of deaconesses dating back to the fourth century, one must not overlook the fact that the selfsame authors who testify to this practice also make clear that the consecration of deaconesses was not the ordination of women to the diaconal office; on the contrary it was a question of a different ecclesiastical ministry.[22]

Why does Müller talk about "liturgical installation"? Does he not know that the Greek sources speak of "ordination," using exactly the same term as for male deacons, priests, or bishops? And who are these "selfsame authors"? How do they testify to the women not being ordained to the diaconal office? If Müller means the authors of the ordination rituals, did he not notice that they demand the "Divine Grace" statement? the presence of the clergy? the setting within the eucharist? the calling down of the Holy Spirit for the imparting of the diaconate? the double imposition of hands? the bestowal of the diaconal stole? in other words, everything needed to make sure that the women received a full sacramental diaconate? Do we not rather hear a clear echo of Martimort's words, "A deaconess was in no wise a female deacon. She exercised a totally different ministry from that of the deacon"?[23]

At times, the appeal to Martimort is made directly: "Martimort shows that the office of the deaconess in the early Church was not understood in a sacramental sense."[24] Müller obviously relies totally on Martimort's conclusions. But the disciple is worse than his master. For Müller, who has not bothered to look at the original sources, can make the outrageous statements quoted above which Martimort, even in his darkest moments, would never dare utter.

Historical ignorance and dogma hand in hand

Now all this would not be so serious if Gerhard Ludwig Müller were no more than a misguided scholar. However, he is a member of the International Theological Commission that advises the Vatican Congregation for the Doctrine of the Faith. He is also chairman of a subcommission appointed to study the diaconate of women. On December 11, 2001, he stated the following about the early women deacons:

> The deaconess in the early Church was not a woman who performed the ministry of a deacon, but someone clearly distinguished from that in her activities. She did nothing done by priests or male deacons. All she did was guard the doors of the church and be present at the baptism of adult women for reasons of propriety. Deaconesses read the Gospel at the hourly prayers in their convents and, when no priest or male deacon was available, took consecrated hosts from the tabernacle and distributed them to the nuns.

In the Syrian and also Byzantine areas we have testimonies of a liturgical installation of deaconesses, similar to that of readers and subdeacons, with the bishop imposing his hands on them to bless them and say a prayer for them.…

To reintroduce the diaconate of women for today would be no more than an amusing anachronism.[25]

Why did Gerhard Ludwig Müller not bother to study the sources, apart from his blind reliance on Martimort? Müller's real reason is a theological one, a conviction that a priori rules out a sacramental ordination of women. This is what he said in the same interview:

It is not possible to separate the diaconate of women from the priesthood of women. This is because of the unity of the sacrament of orders which has been underlined in the deliberations of the Theological Commission. They cannot be measured with a different yardstick.

The reason why the Church does not ordain women is not that they are lacking some spiritual gift or natural talent, but because — as in the sacrament of marriage — the sexual difference of and relation between man and woman contain in themselves a salvific symbolism. This symbolism expresses the salvific dimension of the relation of Christ and his Church.

We must start from the unity of the three degrees of holy orders. Then we see that, since the deacon, just as bishop and priest, acts on behalf of Christ, head and bridegroom of the Church, it is obvious that only a man can represent this relation of Christ and the Church.[26]

In other words, he maintains that the women deacons of the past *could not* be true deacons because that would contradict the nature of women. A woman cannot represent Christ, not even as a deacon. And admitting a true historical diaconate of women would imply admitting the possibility of women being ordained.

An honest appraisal is called for

It is not my intention here to discuss the traditional reasons for which women were excluded from the ministries. Research shows that the underlying causes were cultural, mainly the dominance of men and the fear of menstruation. In the course of time these cultural grounds were justified with spiritual explanations: "Women are punished for Eve's sin." "Jesus did not choose a woman among the apostles." "Paul forbade women to teach." "Being imperfect human beings, women cannot represent Christ," and so on. Of great influence was also Roman law, according to which women could not hold any public responsibility, a principle that became part of Church law. The evidence for all this can be found in my books *Did Christ Rule Out Women Priests?*[27] and *The Ordination of Women in the Catholic Church: Unmasking a Cuckoo's Egg Tradition.*[28]

It is true that these cultural obstacles also hampered the full flowering of the women's diaconate. In the West it impeded its establishment almost completely. And in the Greek-Byzantine area it imposed restrictions on women deacons. Even if propriety would have allowed it, women deacons could not so easily, in normal circumstances, assist the bishop or priest during the eucharist at the altar. Women deacons acted under the authority of priests, or of male deacons. They were not allowed to teach or preach in public. But these restrictions did not obstruct their receiving the full sacramental ordination to the diaconate.

The measuring of the diaconate by its relationship to a sacrificial priesthood and by its involvement in eucharistic ministry dates from the early Middle Ages. In the early Church the "deacon" was what the word says: a "servant," a "helper," assisting the bishop in a wide variety of ministries:

> This is why, O bishop, you must appoint righteous workers, helpers who will cooperate with you in leading others toward salvation. Choose some persons who most please you and institute them as deacons: a man for the administration of the many necessary tasks, but also a woman for ministry among

the women. For there are houses where you may not be able to send a deacon, on account of the pagans, but to which you will be able to send a woman deacon. And also because the service of a woman deacon is required in many other domains.[29]

If we allow the facts to speak for themselves, instead of imposing our own theological straightjacket on them, it is clear that, in spite of all its cultural prejudices, the early Church did admit women to the full diaconate. Their ministry required close cooperation with the bishop or priest in administering key sacraments: baptism and the anointing of the sick. The early Church judged that this ministry among women required a truly sacramental ordination. Theologians and Church leaders should start from an acknowledgment of this reality.

14

How certain are our conclusions?

IN THEOLOGICAL PUBLICATIONS, as well as in popular articles, the old misconceptions regarding women deacons have taken root. The authors will report that research has clearly shown "deaconesses received just a Church blessing." Or they point out that their ordination "is *controversial* among scholars." "Some scholars maintain that women *were* sacramentally ordained as deacons, but this is *only a theory* that has never been proved." End of the debate. You can wash your hands. The facts can be dismissed, or can they?

The truth of the matter is that initial mistaken impressions are erased only with difficulty. Scientists as well as sociologists are familiar with such *myth bonding*. The hunt for UFOs is a case in point. From the 1950s, people in the United States began to see strange shining objects flying in the sky. Many of these sightings can now be linked to test flights of highly secret planes of new design flown from "Area 51," based on information released only recently by the U.S. Air Force. Military personnel were aware of this link, but they allowed the UFO fairy tale to spread in order to protect the secrecy of their new aircraft. The same happened in Russia. Between 1960 and 1990, fifteen hundred(!) spy satellites were launched from a secret base at Poposchkin, which could at times be seen as gliding lights in the skies of northern Europe. But knowing this origin of the "unusual objects" has not killed off the enthusiasm of UFO observers. They continue to cling to their fairy tale with dogged determination. They swear by their "eyewitness accounts" and exhibit flashes recorded on photographic film.

In 1958, while studying theology in London, I challenged one of my professors, who rejected evolution out of hand. "We have 94 percent of biological features in common with chimpanzees," I said. "Skulls of early humans have been found hundreds of thousands of years old.... " (That was the state of science at the time.) "Evolution is just a theory," he replied with scorn. "Nothing has been proved." I was astonished to read later on that this was exactly the reply Bishop Samuel Wilberforce had given to Thomas Huxley almost a hundred years earlier, in 1860, during their famous public debate on evolution in Oxford University!

While I was guiding a group of Catholic pilgrims to the Holy Land, the question cropped up again. Standing on the ancient ruins of Beth-Shan, I mentioned that the city was at least ten thousand years old. "But the world was created four thousand years before Christ!" someone objected. So I tried to explain how the creation stories should be read, and then the biggest surprise came. One senior Catholic priest, who had held key posts in his diocese, piped up: "Don't talk about evolution. It is only a theory; it has never been proved!" This happened in 1995! The six-day creation myth is not dead. It is almost impossible to erase key myths to which people have bonded.

I can sympathize with fundamentalist Christians who, faithful to their literal reading of Genesis, insist on running schools where their children will be taught six-day creation as an equal theory — though imposing such education on others is not acceptable. What I would find totally irresponsible is for Christian authors to continue the myth that "evolution is only a theory that has never been proved." And the same applies to the Martimort myth. The fact that women deacons were given a full "sacramental" ordination is no longer just a theory. It has been proved.

Certainty about the sacraments

It may also be worthwhile to remind ourselves that we are not dealing here with just an academic fact, of passing historical interest. We are talking about the life of the Church. Where would the Church be if the validity of its sacraments can so easily be challenged?

I was ordained a priest in 1959, together with twenty-seven others. We have presided at many eucharists, heard many confessions, anointed many sick persons. Suppose our ordination had been invalid. Then, according to the logic of present-day theology, all those sacraments would have been administered invalidly. So it is vital for us to be certain that our ordination has been a true sacrament. But what if Archbishop Godfrey, who ordained us, had funny ideas about the priesthood? What if he disliked Dutchmen and harbored the secret intention not to ordain them? What if, when imposing his hands, he did not touch my head fully? What if, when he invested me with the chasuble, he did not notice it actually was a subdeacon's dalmatic? The Church has had to deal with many such doubts in its long history, and the reply has always been consistent: all that is needed is *practical* certainty. Such practical certainty is established when it is clear that the ordaining bishop performed the traditional rites as well as he could and was seen to "want to do what the Church wants to do" when imparting ordination.[1]

Allow me to give some examples to illustrate this principle. Accidental changes in the form or matter do not invalidate the sacrament. For instance, what happens if an uneducated person makes mistakes in the words, such as: "I *wash* you in the name of, etc."; or: "in the name of Fathra, Sonna, and Spirita"; or "in the name of the Father, Son, and Holy Spirit and in honor of the Blessed Virgin"? Baptism would be valid if the person intends to do what the Church does, as Pope Zachary wrote to St. Boniface in a letter dated July 1, 746.[2]

Again, from the Middle Ages theologians have debated about what exactly is required with regard to the intention of the minister. If everything depends on his or her internal intention, how can we ever know whether he or she administered the sacrament validly or not? Once more the principle of practical certainty has been reiterated in Church decisions. Pope Leo XIII wrote:

> The Church does not judge someone's mind or intention itself, since this is something interior, but it has to judge [the intention] by how it manifests itself externally. Well, if a person in the

administration of a sacrament applies the proper matter and form in a serious and correct manner, then by that fact itself the person is judged to do what the Church does.[3]

Therefore we only need to know whether the ordaining bishop performed the traditional rites as well as he could, spoke the acknowledged ordination prayers, and generally was seen to "want to do what the Church wants to do" when ordaining deacons. This, as we have seen throughout this book, we can easily establish with regard to women deacons. The bishops clearly followed the ceremonies, spoke the prayers, and indicated by the rites that they intended to ordain these women *as deacons*. These women were, therefore, validly ordained deacons. If their ordination was not valid or not a sacrament, neither was that of the male deacons.

"Wait," I hear a dogmatic theologian object. "But women are not valid matter for ordination. Ordaining a woman can never be valid." This shows exactly the prejudice which we are trying to expose. Bishops in the early Church may have believed women could not validly be ordained priests or bishops, but they obviously were convinced this did not apply to the diaconate. General Church councils sanctioned the women's diaconate. The whole Byzantine part of the Church imparted to women the same sacramental diaconate it imparted to men. The bishops who ordained them were convinced this was a true diaconate. It surely cannot be maintained that this was an error affecting half the Church for at least seven centuries, involving tens of thousands of ordained women deacons and all the Christian communities they served?

The practice of the Greek-Byzantine part of the Church, sanctioned by universal Church councils, constitutes an undeniable part of Church tradition. "Tradition manifests itself in the life of the Church, namely, in practices, liturgical or otherwise, that by common custom are admitted in the Church, even if they are not explicitly expressed in its infallible teaching authority."[4] "In her teaching, *life and worship,* the Church perpetuates and hands on to all generations all that she herself is, all she believes" (Vatican II).[5] The ordination and ministry of women deacons for so many centuries in the greater half of the Church forms an inalienable part of the Church's sacred tradition. It is not just a negative tradition; it establishes something the Church *has done*. And, as Bishop Kallistos Ware has observed and as we have already seen, from what the Church *has done*, we can deduce what it believes *can* be done:

> In the Byzantine rite the liturgical office for the laying-on of hands for the deaconess is exactly parallel to that for the deacon; and so on the principle *lex orandi, lex credendi* — the Church's worshipping practice is a sure indication of its faith — it follows that the deaconess receives, as does the deacon, a genuine sacramental ordination: not just a χειροθεσια but a χειροτονια.[6]

The assessment of scholars

A vast majority of scholars who have taken the trouble to study the evidence firmly support the sacramentality of the women's diaconate in the Byzantine era. Since in academic questions, it is not just numbers that count, but the expertise of the authors, I have tried to sketch this in the short survey that follows. The details I provide about the authors is not complete, or totally up-to-date. I hope that what I have given suffices to somehow indicate their professional competence. It should also be remembered that all these authors have written lengthy expositions on women deacons. I quote only a brief excerpt from each.

Evangelos Theodorou, Orthodox theologian, professor of theology, University of Athens, Greece. Specialized on ancient women deacons, starting with the classic publication *Champions of Christian Love: The Women Deacons through the Centuries* (1949):

> The *cheirotonia* [ordination] of women deacons is imparted only by a bishop with prayer and the imposition of hands. Always and everywhere, until the end of the Byzantine period, it

required a liturgical ceremony which corresponded to the *cheiro-tonia* of male deacons.... The ordination of the woman deacon is absolutely uniform with the ordination of the orders of the higher clergy.[7]

Roger Gryson, professor of theology and church history, Louvain, Belgium. Editor of a new edition of the *Vetus latina*. Books: *Le prêtre selon Saint Ambroise* (1968), *The Ministry of Women in the Early Church* (1976), *Les scolies ariennes du Parisinus latinus 8907* (1980), *Commentaires de Jerôme sur le prophète Isaïe* (1993), etc.:

The evidence is not isolated. It appears in a series of concordant testimonies tending to prove that, in the milieu termed "Syrian-Byzantine," from the end of the fourth century in any case, women deacons received an ordination analogous to that of men deacons, and, as a consequence, if one refers to the concepts of modern theology, it was a sacramental ordination. Since this is not a marginal fact or a fantasy rejected by legitimate authority, but, on the contrary, an institution peacefully accepted by a large part of Christianity for several centuries, one can deduce from it, it seems to me, that when the Church judges it relevant, women can receive the sacrament of orders for a ministry of the diaconal type, whose limits the Church can establish.[8]

Cipriano Vagaggini, professor of liturgy, St. Anselm's University, and lecturer, Oriental Institute, both in Rome. Member of the Vatican's International Theological Commission:

Women deacons were ordained at the foot of the altar inside the sanctuary in clear and deliberate opposition to what was done at the ordination of readers, subdeacons, or other "offices." Other specific ceremonies of the ordination of Byzantine women deacons point in the same direction: the moment of ordination, the use of the "Divine Grace" formula, the horarion, the communion after the male deacons from the hands of the bishop in the sanctuary, the fact of receiving the chalice from the bishop.... With all this it is certain, in my view, that within the history of the one undivided Church, the Byzantine tradition has affirmed that, in nature and dignity, the ordination of the woman deacon belongs to the group "bishop, priest, deacon" and not to the group "reader, subdeacon."[9]

Peter Hünermann, professor of theology at Tübingen, Germany. Former president of the Catholic Theological Association of Europe. Books: *Streitgespräch um Theologie und Lehramt* (1991), *Wissenschaft, kulturelle Praxis, Evangelisierung* (1993), *Das neue Europa* (1993), *Jesus Christus, Gotteswort in der Zeit: Eine systematische Christologie* (1994), *Ekklesiologie im Präsens: Perspektiven* (1995), *Gott, ein Fremder in unserm Haus? Die Zukunft des Glaubens in Europa* (1996), *Papstamt und Ökumene: Zum Petrusdienst an der Einheit aller Getauften* (1997), *Das Zeite Vatikanum: Christlicher Glaube im Horizont globaler Modernisierung* (1998), etc.:

Exactly as the [male] deacons, the women deacons were chosen and ordained by the bishop.... The ordination formulas, the ceremonies — including the laying-on of hands, the handing over of the stole, etc., all of which are retained for women candidates, show that here it is a matter of ordination regarded as on a par with the ordination of a male deacon, i.e., an ordination in the strictest sense, not something like a blessing. The formally sacramental character of this ordination cannot be questioned.[10]

Abraham Andreas Thiermeyer, lecturer in theology and liturgy, Oriental College, Eichstätt, Germany. Book (with others): *Enlogema: Studies in Honor of Robert Taft* (1996):

The ordination of the woman deacon is performed by the bishop through a laying-on of hands and a prayer. It is public, in front of the altar inside the sanctuary, as the ordination of bishops, priests, and male deacons.... The ordination takes place during the eucharist, after the anaphora. An ordination marker, for bishop, priest, and deacon, is the formula

ʽη θεα χαρις. . . . The woman deacon is vested by the bishop with
the diaconal stole and receives the chalice. . . . On account of
these facts, it must be stressed that the woman deacon had a
certain "empowerment over the eucharist." She ranked immediately after the male deacon. She belongs to the clergy. She
receives την ʽιεραν χειροτονιαν, "the sacred ordination," and
so belongs to "the class of ordained persons," ʽη ʽιερα ταξις,
and participates, to use the terminology of Justinian law, in the
ordained priesthood — ʽη ʽιερωσυνη.[11]

Peter Hofrichter, dean of church history and patrology at Salzburg
University, Austria. Books: *Nicht aus Blut, sondern monogen aus
Gott geboren* (1978), *Im Anfang war der "Johannesprolog"* (1986),
Wer ist der "Mensch von Gott gesandt" in Joh 1,6? (1990), *Mod-
ell und Vorlage der Synoptiker: Das vorredaktionelle Johannes-
evangelium* (1997, 2002):

> We should not be surprised about variations in the sources. Dif-
> ferences in ordination rites and in tasks were conditioned by
> culture. Also as a deacon, a woman of late antiquity was sub-
> ject to civil and sacral pressures. . . . Unlike the Syro-Byzantine
> realm, the West had no tradition of women deacons to refer back
> to which explains its absence there. . . . The Apostolic Constitu-
> tions and the Byzantine ordination rite establish beyond doubt
> that women were "sacramentally" ordained deacons.[12]

Anne Jensen, professor of ecumenical theology, history of early
Christianity, Graz, Austria. Books: *Gottes selbstbewußte Töchter:
Frauenemanzipation im frühen Christentum?* (1992), *Thecla: Die
Apostolin. Ein apokrypher Text neu entdeckt* (1993), *Diakonat: ein
Amt für Frauen in der Kirche* (ed. 1997), *Was verändert Feministische
Theologie?* (ed. 2000):

> Could we, in view of the available facts, still share Aimé Georges
> Martimort's opinion that the deaconess had nothing in common

with the male deacon except for the title? It is clear we cannot. The deaconess was truly a female deacon. Her ordination differed only in accidentals from that of her male colleague.[13]

Dirk Ansorge, lecturer in theology and history of religion, Wolfsburg Katholische Akademie, Essen, Germany. Books (with others): *Raum und Transzendenz* (on church architecture, 1998), *Raumerfahrungen* (1999), *Wegmarken europäischer Zivilisation* (2001):

> Toward the end of the fourth century the ancient Church had developed a sophisticated theology of ecclesiastical ordination [χειροτονια/χειροθεσια, etc.]. Gregory of Nyssa compares the effect of ordination to that of the words of *epiclesis* in the eucharist.... When bishops ordained women deacons with the imposition of hands, they were undoubtedly aware of administering the kind of ordination that channelled the grace of the Holy Spirit in an effective and permanent manner. Such an act can only be evaluated as having been a "sacrament."[14]

Christoff Böttigheimer, professor of theology, Catholic University of Munich, Germany. Expert on ecumenism and sacramental theology:

> There existed in the ancient Church a sacramental ordination of women deacons that should be grouped together with that of bishops, priests, and male deacons. It corresponded to the ordination of the male deacon. In today's terminology it should be assessed as having been a sacrament. In the light of this finding of doctrinal history, namely, that for almost a thousand years the Church possessed a female diaconate as a ministry that was imparted through sacramental ordination, no doctrinal objections can be raised against admitting women to the diaconate.[15]

Kyriaki Karidoyanes FitzGerald, Orthodox theologian, lecturer, organizer of the international theological conferences of Orthodox Women in Damascus (1996) and Istanbul (1997). Books: *Women*

Deacons in the Orthodox Church (1998), *Orthodox Women Speak* (1999), and *Happy in the Lord: The Beatitudes* (2000):

> While the Byzantine deaconess received a genuine ordination, it is clear that this still did not imply she had any "priestly" (i.e., officiating) responsibilities. As with a male deacon, the woman deacon's ordination was not an ordination to the presiding priesthood, but rather, this was an ordination to 'ιαρα διακονια, priestly (or sacred) ministry.... The diaconate is to be seen as a complete and analogous order of the ordained ministry that has its own unique integrity.[16]

Phyllis Zagano, associate professor, Boston University. Books: *Religion and Public Affairs* (1987), *On Prayer* (1994), *Twentieth-Century Apostles* (1999), *Things New and Old* (ed. 1999), *The Exercise of the Primacy: Continuing the Dialogue* (ed. 2000), *Holy Saturday: An Argument for the Restoration of the Female Diaconate in the Catholic Church* (2000):

> There remains clear evidence from Tradition that women were solemnly ordained to the apostolate. To deny that women were sacramentally ordained as deaconesses is to deny as well the sacramental ordination of their male counterparts.... Despite popular arguments to the contrary the majority of scholars agree that women were ordained and ordained in the present understanding of the reception of orders.[17]

Dorothea Reininger, theologian, Network Women's Diaconate. Her 736-page dissertation at Mainz University, *Diakonat der Frau in der einen Kirche* (1999), won the Kurt Hellmig award of Regensburg University in 2000:

> The least conclusion we can draw is that rejecting the reintroduction of women's diaconate on doctrinal grounds or on the *ius divinum* (divine law) would be a novelty in the history of the Church. Even if Tradition does not impose the admission

of women to the ordination of the sacramental diaconate with binding force, it does not oppose it either. Whenever it will become opportune to reinstall the female diaconate from a pastoral point of view, the basis for such a step from Scripture and Tradition is there.[18]

Other authors, of no less distinction, have come to the same conclusion. To mention but a few: Yves Congar,[19] Jean LaPorte,[20] Herbert Frohnhofen,[21] Marie-Josèphe Aubert,[22] Andreas Christof Lochmann,[23] Pia Luislampe,[24] Arlene Swidler,[25] Nancy Reynolds,[26] Charles Meyer,[27] Elisabeth Behr-Sigel[28] and Valerie Karras.[29]

Tackling the root problem

Surveying the positive assessment by all these prominent scholars we may ask again: how is it possible for scholars such as Aimé-Georges Martimort and Gerhard Ludwig Müller to arrive at such a totally opposite judgment? I have already shown in the previous chapter that we can uncover an unmistakable "systematic bias" in their writings. These scholars interpret the historical data in the light of their own hermeneutics. As we have seen, Martimort is convinced we can speak of the true sacramental ministry of the diaconate only if the ordinand is given the task of serving at the altar. Müller acknowledges only one sacrament of holy orders, with the diaconate as a first step to a priestly ministry that lies totally outside the reach of women.

May we also, perhaps, infer that with these scholars, and with others who argue like them, it is nontheological considerations and factors of institutional power that play a decisive role: a fear of change, a frantic concern to defend the existing framework of ministry and hierarchy? Could these drive them, consciously or unconsciously, to their selective and tendentious interpretation of the historical facts? Could we be facing an ideological legitimation of the traditional structures of the Church's ministries? Perhaps, even regarding the assessment of the historical diaconate of women, everything boils down to a confrontation of underlying visions of Church and ministry.

Conservative theologians might free themselves by examining their medieval consciences. This is what St. Bonaventure (1217–74) wrote regarding women deacons and how it relates to the wider question of women's admission to holy orders:

> As to whether women are capable [of Orders], there is doubt [among theologians]. Clearly it was the opinion of certain people, called Cataphrygians, that women are capable, and [theologians] not only rely on authorities of past times, but they adhere to the authorities of the canons and bring them out to support themselves, canons in which it is shown that women of old had received Orders. For it states in the twenty-seventh Cause Question 1 [canon 23 of the law book of Gratian]: "We have decided that a deaconess should not be ordained before the age of forty" [Council of Chalcedon]. And in the same Question, "If anyone ravishes or disturbs a deaconess" [from a law of Theodosius], and similarly in Distinction thirty-two [of the law book of Gratian], mention is clearly made of a presbytera [which could mean "female priest" in Latin].
>
> But surely if we pay attention to what is said in Distinction thirty-two, *Presbyteram*, etc., it is shown there that widows and older women, and matrons were called *presbyteras*; and from this it is gathered that the women who communicated with the deacons in reading the homily were called deaconesses. They received some kind of blessing. Therefore in no way should it be believed that there were ever women promoted to sacred orders according to the canons [i.e., laws of the Church].[30]

If we read Bonaventure with an open mind, it is clear that he is completely ignorant of who the ancient women deacons really were, what ministry they exercised, and how they were ordained. But would he not have conceded that women too are capable of holy orders if he had known the facts as we know them today?

It was medieval thinkers who constructed the theological framework that underpins the structures of ministry and hierarchy that we still have today. They molded the sacrificial focus of the priesthood, the feudal power-structures of the Church, the exclusion of women from all authority based on Roman law which they had made the basis of Church law. Their thinking was based on a literalist under-standing of scripture and an appalling ignorance of the Church's rich tradition. Why should we defend the ruins of their antiquated ideology rather than find out what God really wants for his Church?

15

Facing up to the past, for the sake of the future

ANY WOMEN in the Church are already exercising diaconal ministries. They instruct people and prepare them for baptism, confirmation, first communion, and marriage. They give retreats and offer spiritual direction. They preach and conduct church services on Sundays. They look after orphanages, charities, and social institutions. As parish assistants they carry wide-ranging pastoral responsibilities. Why refuse sacramental grace to those women when their ministries, in fact, exceed the tasks permitted to the women deacons of ancient times?

And I do not want to remain with the diaconate. The official Church has to examine its conscience and wake up to the fact that there are no valid reasons for excluding women from any holy order, including the priesthood and the episcopacy. The oft repeated statement that "the Church has never admitted women to holy orders" has been exposed as a fallacy.[1] The undeniable historical reality is that women *were* admitted to the full and sacramental diaconate. This has immediate consequences, both for theology and for the future of the Church.

The truth of historical fact always wins in the end

This is not the first time that theological authority clashes with scientific fact. Galileo Galilei had discovered satellites around planets, and this convinced him that the earth is a satellite of the sun. The earth turns around the sun, not the other way about! He was summoned to Rome in 1633 to stand trial as a heretic. He erected his telescope on the roof of the Holy Office and asked his cardinal judges to look through it and see the satellites around Jupiter for themselves. They refused. They said they could read in Scripture that it was the sun that moved around the earth; they did not need a telescope. They based themselves on a story in Joshua 10:12–13: "Joshua cried: 'Sun, stand still! . . . ' And the sun stood still in the middle of the sky and delayed its setting for a whole day." And had Jesus not said, "The Father causes his sun to rise over evil men as well as good" (Matthew 5:45)? They threatened Galileo with torture and forced him to retract his views in public. "The statement that the earth is not the center of the world; that the earth is not immovable, but that it moves, and moves with the movement of a full day is absurd, philosophically false, and theologically erroneous in faith."[2]

Earlier Galileo had written, "It is not in the power of any creature, not even of the highest religious authority, to make statements true or false, otherwise than if of their own nature and in actual fact they are true or false."[3] They were prophetic words. Galileo has been proved right a million times over. No one today would side with those cardinals of the Holy Office. Theological prejudice lost. Facts won. Theologians are tempted to deny inconvenient facts by clever interpretations, intricate definitions, warped reasonings and interminable objections. If they wield authority, they may attempt to suppress open inquiry and free discussion. At the end of the day, it is a lost battle. How long will it be before the theologians of the Vatican Congregation for the Doctrine of the Faith will be made to admit their mistaken view? But this is not all.

Respecting people in historical fact

As a community of faith we depend on the reliability of the relationships and institutions that we as a Church, as any other social organization would, have built up in time. We have to go by signs and symbols, and by sacraments, to give us stability in all this. What would happen to a diocese if anyone could just deny or ignore the ordained status of the bishop, or of the parish priest? Would our whole Christian trust in each other and respect for each other not crumble?

Communism in Russia applied the mechanism of historical denial as a conscious weapon to destroy institutions it did not like. Churches were converted into warehouses, official histories were rewritten to expunge the record of great spiritual leaders. Tombs of unwanted ancestors were demolished and the records of artists, writers, and saints removed from museums and libraries.

Aimé-Georges Martimort will not have realized the dangerous trend he initiated with his inability to accept the existence of sacramentally ordained deacons. Church authorities who rely on him should reflect on the consequences of their words and actions.

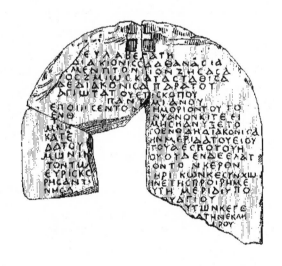

Socially, the Church is a voluntary organization, and its members may well quit if they feel they, or their ancestors, are not respected as persons, simply to suit an ideological theory. And how would the deacons of old feel about seeing their diaconate disowned? I think of formidable ladies like Athanasia in Delphi, Greece, of the fifth century. Her tombstone (see the illustration above) carries this message:

The most devout deaconess Athanasia, established[4] deaconess by his holiness Bishop Pantamianos after she had lived a blameless life. He erected this tomb on the place where her honored [body?] lies. If someone dares to open this tomb in which the deaconess has been buried, may he receive the fate of Judas, who betrayed our Lord Jesus Christ.... [5]

Historical precedent and development of doctrine

Since the Middle Ages, it has been commonly assumed in the Church, without any solid ground, that women had been excluded by God from holy orders. I have listed the fourteen standard medieval arguments and discussed them in detail in my book *The Ordination of Women in the Catholic Church: Unmasking a Cuckoo's Egg Tradition*.[6] The time has now come for the Church to leave these outdated reasonings, which were understandable in the masculine cultures of the time, and rediscover its own life, the inner life of the Spirit.

So far it has not been the practice of the Church to ordain women to the priesthood. In this matter, as happened in so many other episodes in its history, the Church has to move forward in what is known as a "development of doctrine," an acknowledgment of new elements in its faith and practice, elements that were present implicitly but not yet openly recognized as such.

We take it for granted now that there are three "Persons" in God, but the Church struggled for three centuries before this doctrine could be expressed with any degree of confidence. As the awareness of Jesus' divinity grew, it had been natural for many to assume a binary nature in God, i.e., of Father and Son. A good amount of binitarian thought can be documented among pre-Nicene writers. Not that Christian thinkers denied the existence of the Spirit; they would argue that the Spirit was identical to either the Father or the Son. Our present doctrine of "Father, Son, *and Spirit* in One God," difficult to properly fathom or explain even now, found final acceptance also through the established practice of baptism "in the name of the Father, *and* the Son, *and* the Holy Spirit."[7]

The primacy of the bishop of Rome, though assumed in the earlier councils of Florence and Trent, was defined as official Church doctrine only by the First Vatican Council in 1870. The final acceptance of this doctrine by the members of the council was not only due to the scriptural passages in which Christ gave special authority to Peter and to the testimonies of Church Fathers. It was confirmed by Church practice, by the fact that at key junctions in its history, the bishop of Rome had acted as the undisputed leader.

Facts count. In civil law, legal precedents have lasting effects. This has also been the case in Church law. The *Corpus iuris canonici*, the body of Church laws that has dominated Church thinking since 1140, is almost totally based on precedents: decisions by local synods, bishops, popes, Church councils. The Roman principle of precedent was expressed in the phrase *stare decisis*, to be faithful to previous decisions. While this can cripple progress in the Church when earlier decisions were based on prejudice, it can also help to overcome limited ways of thinking on the strength of a surprising precedent. Paul VI broke through an ancient, and seemingly inviolable, custom when he granted permission to receive communion on the hand rather than on the tongue. The custom of receiving communion on the tongue had prevailed in the East from time immemorial, and in the West for more than nine centuries. The pope changed the custom on pastoral grounds and on the strength of the fact that "ancient usage once allowed the faithful to take this divine food in their hands and to place it in their mouths themselves."[8]

The unity of the sacrament of holy orders

Already once or twice in the book I have mentioned the fact that some theologians consider the diaconate a ministry that stands on its own, so that any objections to ordaining women to the priesthood would not apply to their being ordained to the diaconate.[9] They are absolutely right in the sense that the diaconate is a separate ministry and was considered as such in the early Church. This is also how it has been reactivated by the Second Vatican Council. Moreover, whereas in the Middle Ages the three major orders were unified in the priesthood, with the focus on eucharistic sacrificial service at the altar, the Second Vatican Council (1962–65) expressly rejected this view. Deacons are ordained "not unto the priestly ministry [*sacerdotium*], but unto a ministry of service [*servitium*]."[10]

However, this real and important distinction between the three ministries does not destroy their sacramental unity. Vatican II speaks of *one* "divinely established ministry which is exercised on different levels by those who from antiquity have been called bishops, priests, and deacons."[11] It thus confirms the unity of the sacrament already proclaimed by the Council of Trent. Vatican II sees Jesus Christ as the main unifying factor of the sacrament. He is the founder, the origin, the source, the main inspiration from which the variety of ministries originates. Bishops, priests, and deacons all participate to various degrees in Christ's saving work, which he continues in the one sacrament of holy orders.[12]

Theologians discuss this unity in more detail. Peter Hünermann, for instance, gives the oneness a Trinitarian dimension. "The unity of these distinct ministries lies in their common source: the grace of God the Father, the mercy of the incarnate Son, and the goodness of the Holy Spirit. Their unity also lies in their common, ultimate purpose: salvation of people."[13] Christoph Böttigheimer sees the bishop as "the construction joint, the focus of the ministry."[14] Theology will no doubt continue to refine its concepts in line with the new impulse received from Vatican II.

However, for the purpose of this book it suffices to note the unity of the sacrament. While the Council of Trent was somewhat ambiguous about the sacramentality of the diaconate, it was reaffirmed clearly by Vatican II, which stated that deacons are ordained and are strengthened by the grace of the sacrament.[15] This unity of the sacrament directly affects the question of women in the ministries. Since women in the past did receive the sacrament of the diaconate, they are obviously capable of receiving holy orders as such; that means also the priesthood and episcopacy.

Ordaining women to the priesthood

Three powerful factors in today's Catholic Church will enable the Church to overcome ancient prejudice and admit women to all holy orders.

1. Scripture teaches unambiguously that all the faithful, men and women, are made children of God and carry Christ's image. All partake in the general priesthood of Christ through one and the same identical baptism:

> [You are] a holy priesthood, to offer spiritual sacrifices acceptable to God through Jesus Christ.... You are a chosen race, a royal priesthood, a holy nation, God's own people. (1 Peter 2:4–10)

> In Christ Jesus, you are children of God, through faith. As many of you as were baptized into Christ, have put on Christ. There is neither Jew nor Greek, neither slave nor free, neither male nor female. For you are all one in Christ Jesus. (Galatians 3:26–28)

This fundamental identification with Christ through baptism gives every Christian, whether man or woman, the fundamental openness to receive all the sacraments, including holy orders. This is *the scriptural factor*.

2. The full content and meaning of revelation is carried in the hearts of the ordinary members of the Church. It is known as the *sensus fidelium*, the "awareness of the faithful." It is also called the "sense of faith" which, as Vatican II teaches, characterizes the people as a whole:

> The body of the faithful as a whole, anointed as they are by the Holy One, cannot err in matters of belief.... For by this sense of faith which is aroused and sustained by the Spirit of Truth, God's People accepts not the word of human beings, but the very Word of God. It clings without fail to the faith once delivered to the saints, penetrates it more deeply through accurate insights, and applies it more thoroughly to life.[16]

The ordinary faithful carry the treasure of faith, and as new circumstances demand, explore its depth and apply it to the new conditions of life. Well, with regard to women priests, research has abundantly documented that, in countries where people receive a proper education, two-thirds of Catholics feel there is no conflict between Catholic faith and the ordination of women to the priesthood. This applies equally to practicing Catholics, teachers at Catholic schools, parish workers, members of religious congregations, and, when they are free to speak, priests.[17] This is *the sense of faith* factor.

3. In the history of the Church it was assumed, mainly on account of the cultural acceptance of the superiority of men, that women could not be ordained to the priesthood. In spite of this the Church, in its Eastern heartland, did ordain women to the diaconate. For at least eight centuries bishop after bishop laid his hands on woman after woman, invoking the Holy Spirit on her, and imparting the full sacramental diaconate with all the ceremonies that designated it as such. Tens of thousands of women deacons served their parish churches. A fragmentary record of their life and work can be found on tombstones, in written documents, in feasts celebrated in their honor. This undeniable historical precedent proves to the Church that women *can receive holy orders*. This is the final and clinching factor, the factor of *historical practice*.

Illustration I. Part of *folium 94r* in manuscript Verona LV. I have chosen this to demon-
strate the extreme difficulty of deciphering some of the manuscripts. For this codex is a
so-called *palimpsest:* For reasons of economy, scribes would try to scrape an earlier text
from the parchment, and write a new one. In this case the older text is more precious,
and fortunately it can still be read. It contains fragments of the Latin translation of
the *Didascalia* (AD 250), written on this parchment during the fifth century. The later
text, written in the eighth century, contained the *Sententiarum* of Isidore of Seville (AD
560–636).[18]

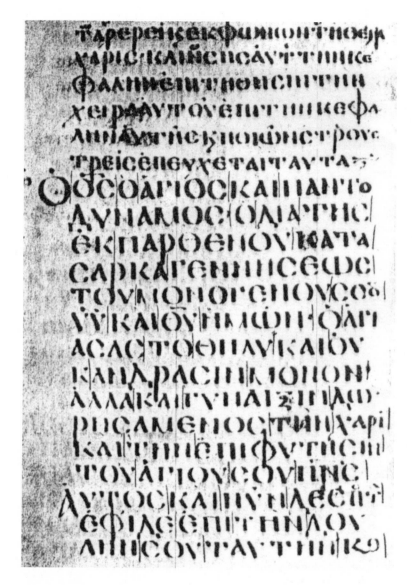

Illustration II. Part of *folium 169v* of Barberini gr. 336. The text was written in 780 using majuscule characters. The rubrics are in smaller characters than the prayer. The text reads, "The archbishop says the 'Divine Grace' with a loud voice, the woman to be ordained bows her head. He imposes his hand on her forehead, makes the sign of the cross on it three times, and prays: 'Holy and Omnipotent Lord, through the birth of your Only Son our God from a Virgin according to the flesh, you have sanctified the female sex. You grant not only to men, but also to women the grace and coming of the Holy Spirit. Please, Lord, look on this your maidservant and dedicate her to the task of your diaconate,'" etc. See p. 175.

Illustration III. *Folium 140b* from MS Barocci 26 (British Museum). Notice the two kinds of script: minuscule and uncial. The text preserves Canon 22 of the Council of Nicea II (787), which reads, "When monks have to eat with women they should pray, and be abstemious and discrete.... For Christ our God instructed us in the Gospel, to cut off the beginning of sin; for not only is adultery rebuked by him, but even thoughts towards adultery when he says, 'Whosoever looks at a woman with lust, has already committed adultery in his heart.' "[19]

Illustration IV. Part of *folium 4r* from Laurentianus VIII, 24. The text was written with minuscule characters in the ninth century. It contains the beginning of the Orations of St. Gregory of Nazianzen (330–89). The inset shows a miniature of Gregory drawn by the monk Xiphilinus, taken from *folium 3v* of the same manuscript. Gregory of Nazianzen preached a eulogy in honor of St. Theosebia, who was a woman deacon and wife of St. Gregory of Nyssa.[20]

THE TEXTS

Women deacons in ancient Greek sources

Judgment on whether the diaconate of women deacons was a true "sacrament" depends crucially on an understanding of the literary sources on which academic research is based. Since many of these sources are not easily available in print, I thought it would be useful to publish them here in English as fully as possible.

Where can the sources be found? The *original sources* are manuscripts, that is, handwritten texts, usually copied on parchment, that are at present preserved in ancient libraries. As I explained in chapter 3, the manuscripts that contain the ordination rite for women deacons can be found in such widely distributed archives as the Bodleian Library in Oxford, the national French library in Paris, the Vatican Library in Rome, the national Greek library in Athens, the monasteries of Grottaferrata in Italy and Mount Athos in Greece, and the library of the Patriarchate of Alexandria in Egypt. The same applies to other manuscripts.

Apart from being dispersed in so many locations, the original manuscripts are also difficult to read, because the writing on them is in archaic Greek majuscule characters which only experts can confidently decipher. Illustrations I–IV (pages 138–141) show what some of the original manuscripts look like. Scholars therefore rely on academic transcriptions of the ancient text into modern Greek script. These scientific publications of the text become the so-called *primary sources* on which scholars can safely base their work. For instance, the text of the Codex Barberini gr. 336 in the Vatican Library was partly published by Jacob Goar in Paris in 1647 and, independently, by Jean Morin in Antwerp in 1685. Only recently has the text been fully published by Stefano Parenti and Elena Velkovska (Rome, 2000).

For the compilation of these texts I have relied on such primary sources, that is, on their scientific transcriptions. I have translated these texts anew from the original Greek wherever it was available — some texts have only come down to us in translation.[1] Obtaining the source books has been a real challenge, requiring research in libraries in London, Oxford, Cambridge, Nijmegen, and Rome. For instance, to publish *Novella 6, 6* (AD 535) in English, I consulted, in the British Library, the monumental publication of Justinian legislation in Greek and Latin by Rudolph Schoell and William Kroll (Berlin, 1899).

Academic translations of ancient texts tend to be word-for-word literal renderings. The stress is on external matching. English sentences are as long as the Greek sentences, and so on. This often results in their sounding odd and failing to convey their full meaning in today's English. During my teaching career in India I had the good fortune of working closely with Professor Eugene Nida, the translation expert of international fame, even joining him in giving workshops for Bible translators. Nida convinced me that accurate translation can and should be done by analyzing the deep structure of the Greek, and dynamically transforming this into the surface structure of the target language.[2] There is no reason why a reliable translation should not be natural, readable, and enjoyable in today's language.

On the other hand, where sensitive Greek terms occur, I have added them after the words within parentheses or brackets. This applies especially to words for "ordination" and for "woman deacon."

Though "deaconess" (διακονισσα) was coined as a synonym in later centuries, the original word for "deacon" (διακονος) could, depending on the gender of the article, stand for the man ('ο διακονος) or for the woman ('η διακονος). As we still do today, the Greeks frequently used the longer form of "woman deacon" (γυνη διακονος).

St. Paul (c. AD 58)

According to scholars, the term "deacon of the church" probably indicates a true ministry, however open-ended the ministry must have been in those early years.[3]

Romans 16:1–2 "Phoebe, our sister, who is a deacon [διακονος] of the church at Cenchreae. Give her a welcome in the Lord worthy of the saints [i.e., the Christians], and help her in anything she may need. She has looked after many people including myself."

Disciple of St. Paul (c. 100)

The letters to Timothy were written by a disciple of Paul, probably to Christian communities in Asia Minor (present-day Turkey). The verses about "the women" do not seem to refer to the wives of male deacons, but to women deacons. The transition is natural in Greek, because the same word διακονοι covers both men and women. To indicate the women, the Greeks would say "διακονοι γυναικες" (deacons women). This interpretation is also followed by the early Greek Fathers (see John Chrysostom and Theodore of Mopsuestia).[4]

1 Timothy 3:8–13 Deacons [διακονους] must be reliable in what they say, not given to wine, not greedy for money. They must hold on to the mystery of faith with a pure conscience. They should be examined first, and may serve as deacons only if there is nothing against them. The women [deacons] in the same way should be respectable, not gossips, but sober and reliable in everything. Deacons [διακονοι] should be husbands of one wife, caring properly for their children and households. Those who have served as deacons [διακονισαντες] with distinction, will achieve a high status and much prospect in the faith that is in Christ Jesus.

Pliny the Younger (112)

Pliny the Younger was a distinguished senator whom the Roman emperor Trajan had appointed to be governor of Bithynia, a province (in present-day north Turkey) suffering from corruption under previous administrations. In this letter Pliny reports on the presence of "Christians," among them two women who, he says, were called "ministrae," which must be a Latin translation of the Greek "diakonoi."

[The Christians who were interrogated] asserted that the sum total of their fault or error had been that they were accustomed to meet on a fixed day before dawn and sing in choir a hymn to Christ as to a god. They bind themselves, they said, by oath, not to commit some crime, but rather to abstain from fraud, theft, or adultery, and not to default on their trust, nor to refuse to return a loan when called upon to do so. When this [function] was over, it was their custom to depart and to assemble again to partake of food — but ordinary and innocent food. Even this, they affirmed, they had ceased to do after my edict by which, in accordance with your instructions, I had forbidden political associations. Accordingly, I judged it all the more necessary to find out what the truth was by torturing two female slaves who were called "deacons." But I discovered nothing more than depraved and excessive superstition.[5]

St. Clement of Alexandria (c. 150–215)

Commentary on 1 Corinthians 9:5: "Have we not the right to take a woman around with us as a sister, like all the other apostles?"

But the latter [the apostles], in accordance with their ministry [διακονια], devoted themselves to preaching without any distraction, and took women with them, not as wives, but as sisters, that they might be their co-ministers [συνδιακονους] in dealing with women in their homes. It was through them that the Lord's teaching penetrated also the women's quarters without any scandal being aroused. We also know the instructions about women deacons [διακονών γυναικών] which are given by the noble Paul in his other letter, the one to Timothy [1 Timothy 3:11].[6]

Origen (185–255)

This is a commentary on Romans 16:1–2: "Phoebe, our sister, who is a deacon [διακονος] of the Church at Cenchreae.... She

has often been a helper both to myself and to many others."
Though the text has been preserved only in Latin, it was
originally written in Greek.

This text teaches with the authority of the Apostle that even women
are instituted deacons in the Church. This is the function which was
exercised in the church of Cenchreae by Phoebe, who was the object of high praise and recommendation by Paul. He enumerated
her outstanding works; she assisted everyone, he said — i.e., she
helped them in their needs — she also helped me in my needs and
my apostolic work with a perfect devotion. I readily compare her action with the hospitality of Lot, who never failed to welcome guests
who presented themselves, and thereby deserved one day to grant his
hospitality to angels. In the same manner, likewise, Abraham, who
always came forward to greet his guests, deserved to have the Lord
with his angels visit him and stay under his tent. Also this pious
Phoebe, while giving assistance and rendering service to all, deserved
to assist and to serve the Apostle himself. And thus this text teaches
at the same time two things: that there are, as we have already said,
women deacons in the Church, and that women, who have given assistance to so many people and who by their good works deserve to
be praised by the Apostle, ought to be accepted in the diaconate. He
also exhorted that the brethren should give consideration to those
who are active in good works in the Church and treat them with
honor [and help them] in whatever they may need, even if it involves
material help.[7]

The Ecclesiastical Canons of the Apostles (c. 250?)

This obscure document contains fragments of second- and third-
century material. The first section quoted seems to refer to
women deacons, while calling them "widows." The identifi-
cation follows from the implicit quote of 1 Timothy 3:8 — a
diaconate passage — and from the allusion to baptismal nu-
dity.[8] The second section, from a different source, mentions the

women's diaconate explicitly and seems to want to explain why women deacons, unlike their male colleagues, do not exercise the role of celebrant.[9] *The text reflects masculine bias, while being at the same time a witness to the existence of the women's diaconate, which it presents as established by the Apostles.*

Canon 21 [The Apostle] Peter said, "Three widows are to be instituted [καθιστανεσθωσαν]. Two will pray for all those who are being tested [catechumens under instruction?] and for the uncoverings in all that is needed [anointing naked catechumens, etc.?]. The other one will look after the women who are suffering illnesses. She must be a good *deacon* [ευ διακονος 'ηι], *reliable,* reporting whatever is needed to the priests, *not given to wine, not greedy for money* [from 1 Timothy 3:8], so that she can stay awake during her ministry at night, or if someone asks her to do other good works. For the first reward of the Lord is good [allusion to Matthew 19:27, and part of diaconate ordination prayer]."

Canons 24–28 Andrew said, "Brothers, it would be useful to institute a diaconate [διακονιαν] for the women." Peter replied, "We have already decided about this. Regarding the offering of the body and the blood we need to be very clear." John said, "You have forgotten, brothers, that when the teacher asked for the bread and the chalice, and he blessed them saying, 'This is my body and blood,' he did not allow the women to stand [as celebrants] with us." Martha said, "That was because of Mary. He saw her smiling." Mary replied, "Not like that. I laughed for he foretold us, when he was teaching, that the weak will be saved through the strong" [*meaning obscure*].[10] Cephas said, "Some things [he taught] you should remember, namely, that it is not fitting for women to pray standing, but rather seated on the ground [*meaning obscure*]."[11] James said, "How then can we establish a diaconate [διακονιαν] regarding women, unless it is a diaconate [διακονιαν] in order to serve women who are in need [of such service]?"

The *Didascalia* of the Apostles (c. 250)

This was a pastoral handbook for bishops, presented as instructions left by the apostles. Originally composed in Greek, it was soon translated into Syriac, Arabic, and Latin. Notice how in chapter 9 the various "ministers" are characterized with images taken from their roles in the liturgy. The bishop sits on his throne — like God the Father. The deacon stands at the altar — serving as Christ did. The priests look like the apostles — whose lifesize images could be seen on the iconostasis. The woman deacon is less prominent — as the life-giving, healing, saving, all-pervading Spirit.[12]

9 §1 Instead of the sacrifices of that [Old Testament] time, now are offered prayers and supplications and thanksgiving. In that time there were first fruits, tithes, sacrifices and gifts; now there is the offering [i.e., the eucharist] presented to the Lord God by the bishops. They are your high priests.

9 §2 The priests and Levites of this present time are the priests and deacons and the orphans and widows — but the high priest and Levite is the bishop. He is the minister of the word and the mediator; and for you he is a teacher as well as your father in God: he gave you birth through water. He is your leader and guide and a powerful king. He guides you in the place of the Almighty. He is to be honored by you as is God himself, because the bishop presides over you like Almighty God.

9 §3 The deacon stands next to you like Christ and you should love him. The woman deacon should be honored by you as [the presence of] the Holy Spirit. Priests ought to be looked up to by you as the apostles are looked up to, and widows and orphans should be considered by you as you would consider the altar of God.

16 §1 This is why, O bishop, you must appoint righteous workers, helpers who will cooperate with you in leading others toward salvation. Choose some persons who most please you and institute

them as deacons: a man for the administration of the many necessary tasks, but also a woman for ministry among the women. For there are houses where you may not be able to send a deacon, on account of the pagans, but to which you will be able to send a woman deacon. And also because the service of a woman deacon is required in many other domains.

16 §2 To begin with, when women go down into the water [of the baptismal font], it is necessary that those going down into the water be anointed with the oil of anointing by a woman deacon. Where no other woman is present, especially where no woman deacon is at hand, it will then be necessary that the man who is performing the baptism anoints the woman being baptized [himself], but he should only put his hand on their heads when anointing them. But where another woman is present, especially a woman deacon, it is not good for women to be seen by a man. Just as in ancient times the priests and kings in Israel were anointed, so must you, with the imposition of your hand, anoint the heads of those receiving baptism — this applies to both men and women.

16 §3 Afterward, whether you yourself are carrying out the baptisms, or whether you have entrusted that responsibility to the deacons and priests, a woman deacon should anoint the women, as we have already indicated. But a man should recite the invocation [ἐπίκλησιν] of the divine names over them in the water.

16 §4 When a woman who has been baptized comes up out of the [baptismal] water, the woman deacon should receive her, and instruct her how to preserve the unbreakable seal of baptism in holiness and purity. For these reasons, we assert that the ministry of a woman deacon is especially required and urgent. For our Lord and Savior was himself served by women deacons, such as Mary Magdalen, Mary, the daughter of James and mother of Joseph, and the mother of the sons of Zebedee, along with still other women.

16 §5 You need the ministry of women deacons for many reasons. The fact is that women deacons are necessary for those houses of

pagans where Christian women are also living. Women deacons can go there and visit those who are ill, serve them in all their needs and, again, to bathe those who are beginning to recover from their illness.

16 §6 Deacons should take bishops as models in their conduct. But they should work even harder than the bishop does. And they should not desire dishonest gains but should be concerned about their ministry. The number of deacons should be in proportion to the number of the people in the congregation. There should be enough so that everyone is known and everyone looked after.

16 §7 Thus, old women whose strength has declined and brothers and sisters who are ill should be able to enjoy from the deacons the service that each one needs. But it is the women [deacons] who should focus on ministry to other women, and the male deacons on ministry to men.

16 §8 The deacon should be ready to obey and submit to the commands of the bishop. The deacon should work and spend himself wherever he may be sent to serve or bear a message to someone. It is necessary that everyone should understand his proper function and be diligent in carrying it out. You [bishop and deacon] should have but one aim, one thought, as one soul in two bodies. And know what ministry means. As our Lord and Savior said in the Gospel, "Whosoever among you wants to be chief, let him be your servant. Just as the Son of Man came not to be served, but to serve, and to give his life a ransom for many."[13]

The Council of Nicea I (325)

The Council had to deal with the followers of Paul of Samosata. Since Paul refused to accept Jesus as the incarnate Son of God, the Council declared all Paulician sacraments invalid: baptism, priesthood, and diaconate. The meaning of the last sentence in Canon 19 is controversial. Did the Council declare that all women deacons, at that time, did not receive the imposition of hands and were not sacramentally ordained? It is also possible to interpret this sentence as restricted to the Paulicians. The Council then rejected in particular the Paulician women's diaconate *because it was not given through imposition of hands.*[14]

Canon 19 "With regard to Paulicians who take refuge in the Catholic Church, it has been decided that they definitely need to be [re]baptized. If, however, some of them have previously functioned as priests, if they seem to be immaculate and irreprehensible, they need to be baptized and ordained by a bishop of the Catholic Church. In this way one must also deal with the deaconesses [διακονισσων] or with anyone established in an ecclesiastical office. We mention the deaconesses [διακονισσων] who are established in this position, because they possess no ordination [χειροτονιαν], so that they are to be reckoned among the laity in every respect."[15]

Epiphanius of Salamis (315–403)

Against Heresies c. 79 There exists for the Church the order of deaconesses [διακονισσων ταγμα], but not for the purpose of performing priestly functions [εις το ʽιερατευειν] or for the purpose of administration. Its purpose is to preserve decency for the female sex, whether in connection with baptism [λουτρου] or in connection with the examination of [women undergoing] suffering or pain, or whenever the bodies of women are required to be uncovered, so that they need not be seen by the men officiating [ʽιερουργουντων], but only by the deaconess [διακονουσης], who is authorized by the priest to minister to the woman at the time of her nudity. Thus it is that the ecclesiastical rule and discipline is wisely and solidly maintained by this particular canon. It is for this reason too that the Divine Word neither permits a woman to speak in the assembly nor allows her to exercise authority over a man. There is a great deal to be said on this subject.

Also, it is necessary to verify with some care that the ecclesiastical organization actually needed only deaconesses [διακονισσων]; the

Church also has widows among whom the older ones are called "seniors" [πρεσβυτιδας], but the Church has never admitted "female presbyters" [πρεσβυτεριδας] or priestesses ['ιερισσας]. In the ecclesiastical order, deacons [διακονοι] themselves have not been given the office of administering any sacrament, but only the office of assisting [διακονειν] those who administer them.[16]

Summary of Faith c. 21 Deaconesses [διακονισσαι] are instituted only for service ['υπηρεσιαν] to women, to preserve decency as required, whether in connection with their baptism or in connection with any other viewing of their bodies. Deaconesses may only have been married once, and they must lead celibate lives or be the widows of a single marriage or else have remained perpetual virgins.[17]

In the next extract (of AD 394), Epiphanius defends himself against the charge of splitting the Church. He had accused Bishop John of Jerusalem with being an Origenist and had, without John's permission, conferred priestly ordination on St. Jerome's brother Paulinian, the abbot of the monastery at Bethlehem, which lay within John's jurisdiction.

Letter to Bishop John, ch. 2 Many bishops in communion with me have ordained priests in my area [i.e., the diocese of Salamis in Cyprus] whom I had been unable to recruit myself. They have sent to me deacons and subdeacons whom I have been glad to receive. Indeed, I have urged Bishop Philo of blessed memory, and Reverend Theoprepus, to make provision for the Church of Christ by ordaining priests in those parishes of Cyprus which, although they were accounted to belong to my see, happened to lie close to them. This for the simple reason that my area is large and sprawling. But for my part I have never ordained deaconesses nor sent them into the territories of others, nor have I done anything to rend the Church. Why, then, are you so angry and indignant with me for that work of God which I have done for the spiritual building up of the brothers, and not for their destruction? Moreover, I have been much surprised at the assertion which you have made to my clergy, that you sent me a message through that reverend priest, the abbot Gregory, that I was to ordain no one, and that I promised to comply.[18]

St. Basil of Caesarea (329–79)

The exact meaning of the following canon is not clear. "Consecration" could mean "made holy through ordination" or "dedicated to continence," which was a requirement for the women's diaconate.[19]

Canon 44 The woman deacon ['η διακονος] who has committed fornication with a pagan [lit. "the Greek"] will be admitted to penance [i.e., not receive communion], and she will not be admitted back to the offering [i.e., the eucharist] until after seven years, and only provided that she has continued to live a chaste life during that time. The pagan ["the Greek"] who after [accepting] faith, commits sacrilege [lit. "temple robbery"] a second time, returns [like a dog] to his vomit. But as to us, we no longer permit the body of a woman deacon [της διακονου], since it has been consecrated [καθιερωμενον="made holy"?], to remain in carnal usage.[20]

St. John Chrysostom (344–407)

The comment refers to 1 Timothy 3:8–11: "The deacons must be serious. . . . The women likewise must be serious, not slanderers, but temperate, faithful in all things."

Homily 11.1 "The women likewise." Paul meant the [women] deacons [τας διακονους]. There are those who think he was talking about women in general. No, that is not the case. It would have made no sense to have inserted here something about women in general. He was referring to those having the dignity of the diaconate [της διακονιας].

"Let deacons be the husband of one wife." This is also appropriately said of women deacons [γυναικων διακονων], for this [monogamy] is necessary, useful, and proper to the highest degree in the Church.[21]

St. Gregory of Nyssa (335–94)

Biographical sources tell us that St. Gregory's wife, Theosebia, was a woman deacon. Here Gregory writes about his sister, Macrina, who spent most of her life in her mother's home. After her mother's death, she converted the family estate into a monastic community. I print here a brief excerpt from Gregory's description of Macrina's life, in which he mentions the local woman deacon who helped him arrange for Macrina's funeral.

On the life of St. Macrina There was a woman in charge of the choir of virgins [i.e., nuns]. She was in the order of the diaconate [εν τωι της διακονιας βαθμωι]. Her name was Lampadia. She declared that she knew Macrina's wishes in the matter of burial exactly. When I asked her about them, she said with tears, "The saint had made up her mind that a pure life should be her adornment, that this should cover her body in life and her grave in death. But so far as clothes to adorn the body go, she procured none when she was alive, nor did she store them for the present purpose. So that not even if we want it, will there be anything more than what we have here, since no preparation is made for this need."

"Is it not possible," I answered, "to find in her cupboard anything to provide for a fitting funeral?" "What cupboard?!" she told me. "You have in front of you all her treasure. There is the cloak, there is the headcovering, there the well-worn shoes on the feet. This is all her wealth, these are her riches. There is nothing stored away in secret places beyond what you see, or put away safely in boxes or in her bedroom. She knew of one storehouse alone for her wealth: her treasure in heaven. There she had stored her all, nothing was laid up on earth." ...

When our work [of preparing Macrina's body] came to an end and the deceased had been covered with the best we had on the spot, the woman deacon ['η διακονος] spoke again, pointing out that it was not fitting that [the deceased] should be seen by the eyes of the virgins robed like a bride [i.e., in a rich, colorful dress]. "But I have kept one of your mother's dark-colored robes," she said. "This I think would do well laid out over her, that her saintly beauty be not decked out with the unnecessary splendor of clothing." Her counsel prevailed, and the robe was laid upon the body.[22]

The *Apostolic Constitutions* (c. 380)

This book was composed from many sources, perhaps at Antioch possibly by a cleric with Arian sympathies. Its influence is disputed. It repeated many of the instructions about women deacons found in the Didascalia. *There are, however, some additions that may reflect local pastoral practice.*[23]

II, 26, 5–7 Let the bishop preside over you as one honored with the authority of God, which he is to exercise over the clergy, and by which he is to govern all the people.

But let the male deacon minister to him, as Christ does to his Father; and let him serve the bishop unblamably in all things, as Christ does nothing of himself, but does always those things that please his Father.

Let also the woman deacon ['η διακονος] be honored by you in the place of the Holy Spirit. Let her not do or say anything without the male deacon; as neither does the Comforter say or do anything of himself, but gives glory to Christ by waiting for his pleasure. And as we cannot believe in Christ without the teaching of the Spirit, so let not any woman address herself to the male deacon or bishop without the woman deacon [της διακονου].

II, 57, 10 Let the doorkeepers stand at the entrances for men, and keep an eye on them. And let the women deacons stand at those of the women.... Let the gates be watched, lest any unbeliever, or one not yet initiated, come in.

II, 58, 1–6 If any brother or sister, man or woman, come in from another parish, bringing letters of recommendation, let the deacon [male or female] be the judge of that affair, inquiring whether they are part of the faithful, and to what church [i.e., parish] they belong? Whether they are defiled by heresy? And besides, whether the party be a married woman or a widow? And when [the male deacon] is satisfied on these questions, that they really belong to the faithful, and are of the same sentiments in the things of the Lord, let him conduct every one to the place proper for him.... Let the woman deacon do the same thing to the women who come in, whether they are poor or rich.

III, 16, 1–2 This is why, O bishop, you must choose co-workers with you for [eternal] life and righteousness, people who are pleasing to God, whom you judge from among all the faithful to be worthy and capable to respond to the requirements of the diaconate [διακονιας]. Choose also a faithful and holy woman deacon for ministry among the women. For there are houses where you may not be able to send a male deacon, on account of the pagans, but to which you will be able to send a woman deacon [γυναικα διακονον], because of the ignorance of the weak. For we need a woman deacon [γυναικος διακονου] for many purposes. To begin with, when women are being initiated [φωτιζεσθαι], the male deacon anoints them first with the sacred oil on the forehead, and after him the woman deacon ['η διακονος] anoints them [over the rest of their body]. For there is [then] no need for women to be seen by men.

III, 16, 4 You therefore, bishop, according to the type [of Christ, the Anointed], shalt anoint the head of those that are to be baptized, whether they be men or women, with the holy oil, to symbolize spiritual baptism. After that, either you, bishop, or a priest who is in your charge, shall baptize them in the water, speaking the sacred calling-down prayer [επικλησιν] over them, mentioning them by [their] name, [the calling down] of Father, and Son, and Holy Spirit. And let the male deacon receive the man, and the woman deacon [ἡ διάκονος] the woman, so that the conferring of this inviolable seal may take place with decency. And after that, let the bishop anoint those who have been baptized with chrism.

III, 19, 1–2 Male deacons should in every respect be blameless, like their bishop, but more hardworking then they are, proportionate in number to the size of the community, so that they can also serve the underprivileged as "workers that need not be ashamed." And let the woman [deacon] be diligent in taking care of the women. Both of them should be ready to carry messages, to travel about, to minister, and to serve, as Isaiah said about the Lord [Christ]: "To justify the righteous, serving many people well." Let everyone therefore know his proper place, and discharge it diligently with one consent, with one mind, as knowing the reward of their diaconate. Let them not be ashamed to minister to those that are in want, as even our Lord Jesus Christ came "not to be served, but to serve and give his life as a ransom for many."

VII, 17, 4 [Only] a chaste, unmarried woman should become a deaconess [διακόνισσα]. Or otherwise, a widow who has been married only once, who is faithful and of good reputation.

VII, 27 A male deacon does not bless [any object], does not give the blessing [at the eucharist], but receives it from the bishop and priest. He does not baptize, he does not offer [the eucharist]; but when a bishop or priest has offered [it], he distributes [communion] to the people, not as a priest, but as one that ministers to the priests. But it is not lawful for any one of the other clergy to do the work of a deacon.

A deaconess [διακόνισσα] does not bless, nor perform what belongs to the office of priests or deacons, but only guards the doors, and ministers to the priests in the baptizing of women, on account of decency.

A male deacon can dismiss a subdeacon, a reader, a singer, and a deaconess [διακόνισσα], if there be any occasion, in the absence of a priest. It is not lawful for a subdeacon to dismiss either one of the clergy or laity; nor for a reader, nor for a singer, nor for a deaconess, for they are the assistants of the deacons.[24]

Ordination rite in the *Apostolic Constitutions*

This is the oldest known text of the ordination to the diaconate, both for men and women. Most commentators consider these ordinations, for both men and women, to have been fully "sacramental" in present-day terms.[25]

VIII, 17–18 Concerning the [ordination of] a [male] deacon, I [the Apostle] Philip give this instruction:

You will ordain a deacon, O bishop, by laying your hands upon him in the presence of all your priests and deacons, and shall say the following prayer:

O God Almighty, true and faithful God, you are generous to all that sincerely call upon you. You are awesome in your designs, and wise in understanding. You are powerful and great. Hear our prayer, O Lord, and let your ears receive our supplication, and cause the light of your face to shine upon this your servant, who is to be ordained [προχειρισάμενος] for you to the diaconate [εἰς διακονίαν]; and fill him with your Holy Spirit, and with power, as you filled Stephen, who was your martyr, who followed the sufferings of your Christ. Make him worthy to discharge the ministry of a deacon properly, steadily, unblamably, and without fault, that thereby he may attain a higher degree, through the mediation of your only-begotten Son, to whom with you and the Holy Spirit be glory, honor, and worship forever. Amen.

VIII, 19–20 Concerning [the ordination of] a deaconess [διακονίσσης], I [the Apostle] Bartholomew give this instruction:

O bishop, you will lay your hands upon her in the presence of the priests, deacons, and deaconesses [διακονισσῶν], and shall say the following prayer:

O Eternal God, the Father of our Lord Jesus Christ, the Creator of man and of woman, you filled Miriam, Deborah, Anna, and Huldah with the Spirit. You did not object to your only-begotten Son to be born of a woman. You ordained [προχειρισάμενος] women to be keepers of your holy gates in the tabernacle of the testimony and in the Temple.

Do now look upon this your handmaid, who is to be ordained [προχειριζομενην] to the diaconate [εἰς διακονίαν], and grant her your Holy Spirit, and cleanse her "from every defilement of body and spirit" (2 Corinthians 7:1), that she may worthily discharge the work which is entrusted to her, to your glory, and to the praise of your Christ, to whom with you and the Holy Spirit be glory and adoration forever. Amen.

Emperor Theodosius (347–95)

The emperor Theodosius I, who first ruled the East of the Byzantine empire, then both East and West, took an active interest in Christianity as a unifying factor in his realm. The following law (AD 390) is extant only in its Latin form. The lawyer who drew up this canon may have been unfamiliar with Eastern Church practice. He seems to have assimilated "deaconesses" and "widows." He was concerned that a priest, who had authority over a women deacon, might claim her inheritance for the Church, at the expense of the family. The law was relaxed soon after (394).

Law XVI, 2, 27 No woman, unless older than sixty years and having children at home, should be transferred to the company of deaconesses according to the precept of the Apostle [Paul; cf. 1 Timothy 5:3–13]. She should [legally] entrust her property to her children if they are capable, requesting the help of a guardian if the children's age demands this, to be administered by them with religious care. She should obtain the income only of her [landed] estate, and she retains full power to keep this, sell this, give this, divide this, and bequeath either what is left of it or what she grants at her death, provided she possesses her free will. Nothing of her jewels or expensive dresses, nothing of gold, silver, and other treasures of a noble household, should she spend under pretext of religion, but she should legally transfer everything totally to her children or relatives or others of her own choice And when she dies, she may not declare any church, any cleric, or any poor person to be her heir.[26]

Pelagius (354–418)

Pelagius was a monk, born in Britain. He is mainly remembered in church history and theology because of his views on free will, sin, and redemption, for which he was condemned as a heretic by various local councils. After having spent time in Rome and North Africa, he settled in Palestine from 412. The reason why we have, by way of exception, included this Latin author in this anthology of Greek sources, is his acquaintance with the women's diaconate as practiced in the East. He identified the "widows" mentioned in the Pastoral Letters as women deacons.

On 1 Timothy 3:11 "The women too should be chaste." He [i.e., Paul] orders that they should be chosen on the same terms as deacons. From this we may conclude that he speaks of those women who are still called "deaconesses" in the East.[27]

On Romans 16:1 "[Phoebe] who is at the service of the church that is in Cenchreae." In the eastern regions one sees women deaconesses [*diaconissae mulieres*], even to this day, serving members of their own sex in baptism and in the ministry of the word. For we find women who teach in private, as Priscilla whose husband was called Aquila.[28]

On 1 Timothy 5:9–11 "Choose as widow a woman who is at least sixty years old, who has only been married once." He wants that only those women be chosen as deaconesses who would be models of life for all.... "As to young widows, avoid them." Avoid proposing them to others in the ministry of the diaconate for fear that they might set a bad example rather than a good one.[29]

Theodore of Mopsuestia (350–429)

The following three extracts are taken from Theodore's commentaries on St. Paul's letters.

On 1 Timothy 3:11 Since Paul was speaking immediately before about deacons, and since this name [deacon] applies also to women given to similar tasks, he quite logically added that the women also should be chaste. This does not mean that the wives of deacons were established in this service, but that any women who were established in it to exercise the same office as the [male] deacons had to be as distinguished in their zeal for virtue as those same deacons...After having mentioned cases of women given the responsibility of the diaconate, a mention which is explicable because of the similarity of the names, [Paul] went on to pick up the thread again of what he had been saying about [male] deacons. And he added: "Let deacons be the husband of one wife."[30]

It is worth adding that we should not be surprised at the fact that he [Paul] does not mention subdeacons or readers here. For these [functions] are actually outside the orders of real ministry [λειτουργια] in the Church. They were created later on by the need of many things that had to be done by others for the good of the multitude of the faithful. That is why the law does not permit them to receive ordination in front of the altar because they do not minister ['ου λειτουργουτ] at this mystery [i.e., sacred service at the altar]. For the readers look after the readings and the subdeacons in the sacristy prepare what is needed for the service of the deacons and look after the lights in church. However, only the priests and deacons perform the ministry of the mystery [at the altar]: the former by fulfilling their priestly role, the latter by ministering to sacred things.[31]

On 1 Timothy 5:9 The apostle [Paul] wanted above all to indicate the age that must be attained by those to be received into the order of widows. Certain people, however, paying little attention to his reason for providing this indication, have wondered if it was possible to ordain women deacons [at a younger age], imagining that women deacons somehow necessarily had to be received into the higher order of widows. These people have not understood that if [Paul] had wished to prescribe such an age rule for ordination, he would certainly have prescribed it first of all for priests and bishops. But this is manifestly not the case. Paul never believed that function should be determined in accordance with age. Timothy, after all, was very young.[32]

Sozomenos (c. 443)

This author was a contemporary of St. John Chrysostom and St. Olympias, and he had direct access to primary witnesses. In his History of the Church *he narrates the turbulent events*

*surrounding John's expulsion from Constantinople and the per-
secution of John's followers. Of great value is his acceptance of
ordained women deacons as a normal feature of Church life.*

Book 8, ch. 9 The enmity of the clergy against John [Chrysos-
tom] was greatly increased by Serapion, his archdeacon. This man
was an Egyptian, naturally given to anger, and always ready to
insult his opponents. The feelings of hostility were further fos-
tered by the advice which John gave to Olympias. Olympias, who
hailed from an elevated noble family, became a widow as a young
woman. Because she was admirably educated in accordance with ecclesiastical law, [Archbishop] Nektarios had ordained her a deacon
[διακονον 'εχειροτονησε]. John noticed that she liberally shared of
her wealth with anyone who approached her. He also saw that she
despised everything but the service of God, so he said to her, "I ap-
plaud your good intentions, but I would like you to know that those
who aspire to the perfection of virtue according to God ought to distribute their wealth with prudence. You, however, have been pouring
gifts on the rich, which is as useless as if you had thrown these things
into the sea. Do you not realize that you have voluntarily, for the sake
of God, dedicated all your possessions to the relief of the poor? You
ought, therefore, to regard your wealth as belonging to your Master,
and to remember that you have to account for its distribution. If you
take my advice, regulate your donations according to the needs of
those who ask for help. Then you will be able to increase the effec-
tiveness of your generosity, and your mercy and most zealous care
will be rewarded by God."[33]

Book 8, ch. 24 Olympias the deacon ['η διακονος] manifested her
strength of character during this time of upheaval [when St. Chrysostom had been exiled and the Hagia Sophia was set on fire by his
followers]. She was dragged before the tribunal and interrogated by
the prefect [of the city, Optatus] as to her motives in setting fire to
the church. She replied, "My past life ought to avert all suspicion
from me, for I have devoted my large property to the restoration of
the temples of God." The prefect alleged that he was well acquainted

with her past course of life. "If that is the case," she replied, "why do you not take the place of the accuser and let someone else judge both of us?" Since the accusation against her could not be substantiated with proofs, the prefect found that he had no ground on which he could justly blame her. So he lessened the charge and began to speak as if he was anxious to give her good advice. He found fault with her, he said, and with the other women, because they refused communion with his [newly appointed] bishop [Arsacius, whom John's followers considered a schismatic usurper]. "There is still time to repent," he said, "and so to change your own situation." All the [other women] deferred to the advice of the prefect out of fear, but Olympias gave this answer: "It is not just that, after having been publicly calumniated, without having had anything proved against me in court, I should be obliged to clear myself of charges totally unconnected with the accusation in question. Let me rather take counsel concerning the original accusation that has been preferred against me. For even if you resort to unlawful compulsion, I will not hold communion with those from whom I have, in conscience, to keep a distance, nor will I consent to anything that is not lawful to the pious." When the prefect found that he could not prevail upon her to hold communion with Arsacius, he dismissed her in order that she might consult her lawyers. On another occasion, however, he again sent for her and condemned her to pay a heavy fine, for he imagined that by this means she would be compelled to change her mind. But she totally disregarded the loss of her property and left Constantinople for Cyzicus.

The priest Tigrius was about the same period stripped of his clothes, scourged on the back, bound hand and foot, and stretched on the rack. He was a non-Greek by race, and a eunuch, but not by birth. He had originally been a slave in the house of a man in authority, and on account of his faithful services had obtained his freedom. He was afterward ordained a priest [χειροτονηθησε πρεσβυτερος], and was distinguished by his moderation and meekness of disposition, and by his charity toward strangers and the poor. Such were the [shocking] events that happened in Constantinople at the time.[34]

Pseudo-Ignatius (fifth century)

This shadowy figure seems to have been a bishop in Syria and follower of Apollinarius, a fourth-century teacher who denied that Christ had a rational human soul, since Christ's mind was divine. Pseudo-Ignatius wrote in the name of the legendary St. Ignatius of Antioch. The interest in this passage lies with the mention of three groups of women: deacons, nuns, and widows.

I greet the women who watch the holy doors, the [women] deacons in Christ [τας εν χριστωι διακονους]. I greet the virgins who have accepted Christ, and whom I brought up in the Lord Jesus. I greet the very chaste widows.[35]

Theodoret of Cyrrhus (393–458)

On 1 Timothy 3:11 "The women likewise," that is to say, the [women] deacons [τας διακονους], "must be serious, not slanderers, but temperate, faithful in all things." What he prescribed for men, [he prescribed] in similar terms equally for women. For just as he required [male] deacons to be "serious," so he required women [deacons] to be serious. Just as he required [male] deacons not to be "double tongued," so he required the women [deacons] to be "not slanderers." Just as he required [male] deacons not to be "addicted to much wine," so he required the women [deacons] to be temperate.[36]

The Council of Chalcedon (451)

This was the fourth general council for the whole Church, attended by 520 bishops from the East and West, including representatives from Pope Leo I. It defined the doctrine of Christ's two natures against the Monophysites, and concerned itself mainly with regulating Church discipline.

Canon 15 "A woman shall not be ordained [χειροτονεισθαι] a deaconess [διακονισσαν] under forty years of age, and then only after strict examination. And if, after ordination [χειροθεσιαν] and active involvement for a time in the ministry [λειτουργια], she shall despise the grace of God and give herself in marriage, she shall be expelled from the community, and so shall the man united to her."[37]

First Synod of Dvin in Armenia (527)

The Church in Armenia was founded by the Greeks. Part of its area belonged to the Byzantine Empire. Later, at the Second Synod of Dvin (554) it would officially become Monophysite, i.e., it would refuse to accept the human as well as the divine nature in Christ. The following canon, decreed when the Armenians were still in communion with the world Church, confirms the ministry of ordained women deacons among them.

Canon 17 During the administering of baptism, [ordinary] women may not serve as if they were women deacons.[38]

Severus of Antioch (465–538)

This Monophysite bishop, who was exiled from Antioch, wrote letters from Egypt to his communities in Syria. Though he is part of the Syriac tradition of the region, he knew the Greek customs well. Moreover, his writings show that his own churches were also familiar with the diaconate of women. Among his letters, four were addressed to individual women deacons: Anastasia, Jannia, Eugenia, and Valeriana.[39] The last two excerpts are from a text written by some "holy fathers" (534) who stood under the authority of Severus, which is the reason why the text is also attributed to him.

Letter 49 The practice of devout women, who live in their own homes, being ordained deacons is very common. It is spread, if I may say so, over the whole world.[40]

Letter 62 In the case of women deacons, especially in convents, ordination is performed less with regard to the needs of the mysteries than exclusively with regard to doing honor. In the cities, however, women deacons habitually exercise a ministry relating to the divine bath of regeneration for the sake of women who are being baptized.[41]

Canon 9 The custom of the East, namely, that the superiors of convents of nuns are women deacons and distribute the sacraments to those who are under their authority, should be preserved everywhere where there is a woman deacon, as long as no pure priest or male deacon is present in the place where the sacraments are dispensed. But if a pure priest or male deacon are at hand, then the superiors should not distribute [communion].[42]

Canon 11 The ordination of a woman deacon will take place according to the custom of the country. Moreover, it is a known fact in the East that the bishop puts an orarion on the shoulder of the ordinand, as he does for the male deacon.[43]

Code of Emperor Justinian I (529–64)

Justinian was Byzantine emperor for almost forty years (527–65). One of his reforms consisted of checking and codifying existing laws. The purpose was not so much to introduce innovations, as to streamline existing legal systems. This also extended to the organization of the Church. We reproduce here Novella 6, 6, part of a decree by which the emperor legislated on Church affairs in 535.

Novella 6, 6 §1 Whatever we have decreed about the venerable [male] clerics, we want also to apply to the God-pleasing deaconesses [διακονισσων], so that they too do not transgress the [right] practice.

§2 First of all, in age they should neither be young, nor in their flowering which could easily lead to transgressions, but from those who have passed their middle age and who are, in harmony with divine rules, more that fifty years old. Only then they merit sacred ordination [χειροτονιας].

§3 And they should be either women confirmed as virgins, or widows who have been the wife of one husband. For we will not allow those who have contracted a second marriage or those who have led a life either reprehensible or even in any way suspect to approach the sacred mysteries and minister to the revered rites of baptism and to be part of other secret rites, which they rightly perform in connection with the venerable mysteries.

§4 When, however, there is some real need as the occasion arises to ordain as deacon [χειροτονηθηναι διακονον] a woman who is younger than the age stipulated above, she may be ordained [χειροτονεισθαι] in some sacred convent and live there where she will have no involvement with men and provided that she is not left to her own devices, but is a modest person who lives a simple life and whose worthiness has been testified to by many people who have lived with her.

§5 But we do not want those women deacons [διακονους] who are called to ordination [χειροτονιαν] after either having been a widow or a virgin, to remain in close association with relatives, friends or "sponsors" — for those who use this kind of name burden their life with a lot of bad suspicion. Rather, they should either live on their own, or only with their parents and children or true brothers or other persons about whom, if someone would presume to suspect evil of them, that person himself would both be judged to be a fool and impious.

§6 Therefore, if something of this nature is said about a woman who would like to receive the ordination to deaconess [διακονισσης χειροτονιαν], namely, that she has some involvement with a person about whom in spite of a good reputation there is some evil suspicion, a woman of this nature should not at all be admitted to the diaconate ordination [χειροτονιαν διακονιας].

§7 For if she commits anything of that kind and has a relationship with someone of the reputation mentioned, although she has been ordained [χειροτονηθοιη], she will lose her diaconate [διακονιας] and both she herself and the man will be subject to this law and all the other laws that punish those who corrupt women.

§8 All those women who will be ordained [χειροτονουμενας] as venerable deacons [διακονους] must, at the time of their ordination [χειροτονιας], both be admonished and be told of the sacred prescriptions in the hearing of all the other venerable women deacons [διακονων] who already exist, so that they preserve the fear of God and resolve to adhere to the sacred rules, so that they also will fear to lose their sacred order ['ιερας ταξεως], in the knowledge that if they will presume to shame their ordination [χειροτονιαν], or leaving their sacred ordination [χειροτονιαν], choose to marry, or elect an entirely different kind of life, they themselves will be subject to the death penalty and their property will be confiscated and given to the sacred churches or monasteries to which they are attached.

§9 But the men who have presumed to either accept them as their wives or to commit fornication with them will themselves be subjected to the sword, and their property will be confiscated by the state treasury.

§10 For if according to the ancient laws those virgins who had been called to their dignity by mistake incurred the condemnation of death when they were corrupted [i.e., the Vestal Virgins], how should we not all the more decree [this punishment] on those women who are glorified by God, anxious as we are to preserve chastity, which is one of the highest ornaments in women and which agrees so much with venerable deaconesses [διακονισσων], so that they both guard what is becoming by nature and preserve what they owe to their priestly ministry [τηι 'ιεροσυνηι].[44]

Novella 131 dates from 545. Notice how the woman deacon, like other members of the clergy, was ordained for a specific church community.

Novella 131, 23, line 23ff. If a bishop, or cleric, or minister of whatever ecclesiastical grade, or deaconess of a church [εκκλησιας διακονισσα], dies without a last will and legitimate heirs, the church in which these [ministers] were ordained inherits [what they owned].[45]

Novella 123 (AD 546) is mainly concerned with judicial matters involving clerics. Concern about public morals affecting the clergy also extended to women deacons. In Novella 123, 13, the emperor had already reiterated that no woman should be ordained a deacon if she was younger than forty years old, or if she had entered a second marriage. See Novella 6, 6, §5–7 with an explanation of the men in a woman deacon's house who would not arouse suspicion.

Novella 123, 30 We do not permit a deaconess [διακονισσα] in any way to live with a man when this might give rise to suspicions regarding her chastity. If she does not observe this rule, the priest who has charge of her should admonish her to expel such a man at all costs from her home. If she is reluctant to do this, she should be relieved of her ecclesiastical ministry ['εκκλησιαστικης 'υπηρεσιας] and of her church income, and relegated to a convent where she should stay for the rest of her life. Her possessions should be divided between herself and her children, if she has any, according to the number of people involved, and the portion that belongs to her should be handed to the convent so that it can look after her. If she does not have children, her property shall be equally divided between the convent and the church in which she had been installed.[46]

Joannes Moschus (before 619)

The following incident is recounted in a collection of inspirational legends, called the Spiritual Meadow. *The author died in 619, but the event is supposed to have taken place a century earlier, while Peter was archbishop of Jerusalem (524–48). The story reveals the attitudes of the time, and testifies to the ministry of women deacons.*[47]

At the monastery of Penthucla was a certain Conon of Cilicia, a priest assigned to [the ministry of] baptism. Since Conon was an old man of high repute, the [monks] appointed him to perform the baptisms. Thus he used to anoint and baptize those who were presented to him for this. But whenever he did anoint a woman, he felt tempted [lit. "scandalized"], and because of this, he wanted to leave the monastery. When he was on the point of leaving, St. John [the Baptist] appeared to him and said: "Have patience, and I will deliver you from this struggle."

One day a young woman from Persia came to be baptized. She was attractive, yes exceptionally gorgeous, so that the priest did not have the courage to anoint her with holy oil. Since she stayed there for two days, Archbishop Peter [of Jerusalem] heard about this. He was concerned about what had happened and wanted to designate a woman deacon [διάκονον γυναῖκα] for this function; but he did not do it, since the place did not permit it. Father Conon packed his bag, left, and said, "I will not stay here any longer."

As he was roaming through the hills, St. John the Baptist appeared to him and said in a soft voice, "Go back to your monastery and I will deliver you from your struggle." Father Conon answered angrily, "Believe me, I will not go back, because you often made a promise and you never kept it." Then St. John calmed him and requested that he sit upon a hill. Then St. John took off [Conon's] clothes, and marked him three times with the sign of the cross below his navel, saying, "Have confidence in me, Father Conon. I wanted you to prove yourself worthy of a reward in regard to this struggle; but since you do not want it, I have nevertheless delivered you from it. But you will not have the reward that would have been coming to you."

Father Conon returned to the monastery where he used to baptize. The next morning he anointed and baptized the young woman from Persia without even knowing that she was a woman. He kept this office for twelve years, anointing and baptizing, without any movement of the flesh and without noticing any woman. This he continued doing till his death.[48]

The Council of Trullo (692)

This was the seventh general council of the Church; it is also known as the Quinisext Council. Convoked by Emperor Justinian II in his Trullus Palace near Constantinople, it was attended by 211 Greek-speaking bishops. Its main purpose was to complete the Council of Constantinople by issuing "canons." The reigning pope, Sergius (687–701), who had not been represented at the Council, refused to sign the decrees, but a century later Pope Hadrian I (772–95) recognized the Trullan decrees.

Canon 14 Let the canon of our holy God-bearing Fathers be confirmed in this particular also; that no one be ordained a priest before he is thirty years of age, even if he be a very worthy man, but let him be kept back. For our Lord Jesus Christ was baptized and began to teach when he was thirty. In like manner let no deacon be ordained [χειροτονεισθω] before he is twenty-five, nor a deaconess [διακονισσα] before she is forty.[49]

Canon 48 If a man is promoted to the episcopal dignity, his wife should by common consent separate herself from his house, and after his ordination to the episcopacy, she should enter a convent far from the bishop's residence. She should be maintained from the bishop's income. And if she is worthy of it, let her be promoted to the dignity of the diaconate [της διακονιας 'αξιωμα].[50]

> **Note.** *During the fifth or sixth century the ordination rites for bishops, priests, male deacons, and female deacons became standardized and fixed.[51] Starting from this point, I print here the rite for women deacons as preserved in eight distinct manuscripts. Italics indicate text that varies from the standardized version.[52]*

Codex Barberini gr. 336, Italy (780)

Written in southern Italy from a Constantinopolitan model, this codex was used by a Greek-Byzantine bishop for ordinations until the early Middle Ages. Nicholas Nicoli bought it, around 1400, and left it to the Florentine Monastery of St. Mark in 1441. Carlo Strozzi probably gave it to Cardinal Francesco Barberini around 1650. It was acquired by the Vatican Library in 1902.[53]

Prayer for the ordination of a deaconess
[ˈευχη ᾽επι χειροτονιαι διακονισσης]

After the sacred offertory, the doors are opened and, before the deacon starts the litany "All Saints," the woman who is to be ordained deacon is brought before the pontiff. And after he has said the "Divine Grace" with a loud voice, the woman to be ordained bows her head. He imposes his hand on her forehead, makes the sign of the cross on it three times, and prays:

> Holy and Omnipotent Lord, through the birth of your Only Son our God from a Virgin according to the flesh, you have sanctified the female sex. You grant not only to men, but also to women the grace and coming of the Holy Spirit. Please, Lord, look on this your maidservant and dedicate her to the task of your diaconate [της διακονιας], and pour out into her the rich and abundant giving of your Holy Spirit. Preserve her so that she may always perform her ministry [λειτουργια] with orthodox faith and irreproachable conduct, according to what is pleasing to you. For to you is due all glory and honor.

After the "Amen," one of the deacons now starts this prayer:

> Let us implore the Lord in peace. For peace from above, let us pray the Lord. For peace in the whole world. For this our archbishop, for his priestly ministry, his reward, his endurance, his peace and salvation, and the work of his hands, let us pray the Lord. For so-and-so [name of the woman] who is to receive

the diaconate and for her salvation. That God who loves people grant her a pure and immaculate diaconate, let us pray the Lord. For our pious emperor who is protected by God, etc., etc.

While the deacon makes these intercessions, the archbishop, still imposing his hand on the head of the ordinand, prays as follows:

Lord, Master, you do not reject women who dedicate themselves to you and who are willing, in a becoming way, to serve your Holy House, but admit them to the order of your ministers [λειτουργων]. Grant the gift of your Holy Spirit also to this your maidservant who wants to dedicate herself to you, and fulfil in her the grace of the diaconate [διακονιας], as you have granted to Phoebe the grace of your diaconate [διακονιας], whom you had called to the work of the ministry [λειτουργιας]. Grant her, Lord, that she may persevere without guilt in your Holy Temple, that she may carefully guard her behavior, especially her modesty and temperance. Moreover, make your maidservant perfect, so that, when she stands before the judgment seat of your Christ, she may obtain the worthy fruit of her excellent conduct, through the mercy and humanity of your Only Son.

After the "Amen," he puts the stole of the diaconate [το διακονικον ὡραριον] around her neck, under her veil, arranging the two extremities of the stole toward the front.

When the newly ordained has taken part of the sacred body and precious blood, the archbishop hands her the chalice. She accepts it and puts it on the holy table.

Sinai Codex gr. 956 (tenth century)

This codex is found in the library of St. Catherine's monastery on Mount Sinai. The monastery is the oldest existing Greek monastery, occupied ever since its foundation under Emperor Justinian I in 527. It has a priceless collection of ancient manuscripts. The codex in question contains liturgical texts that were

*copied in the tenth century from both a model in Constanti-
nople and from another Byzantine model that has not yet been
identified.*[54]

Prayer for the ordination of a deaconess
[ˈευχη ˈεπι χειροτονιαι διακονισσης]

After the sacred offertory, the doors are opened and, before the deacon starts the litany "All Saints," the woman who is to be ordained
is *brought forward*. And *the pontiff says* the "Divine Grace" with a
loud voice *while she* bows her head. And he imposes his hand on her
head, and making three crosses on it says:

> Holy and Omnipotent Lord, through the birth of your Only
> Son our God from a Virgin according to the flesh, you have
> sanctified the female sex. You grant not only to men, but also to
> women the grace and coming of the Holy Spirit. Please, Lord,
> look on this your maidservant and dedicate her to the task of
> your diaconate [της διακονιας], and pour out into her the rich
> and abundant giving of your Holy Spirit. Preserve her so that she
> may always perform her ministry [λειτουργια] with orthodox
> faith and irreproachable conduct, according to what is pleasing
> to you. For to you is due all glory and honor.

After the "Amen," one of the deacons *says the prayer, and while
this happens,* the archbishop, still keeping his hand on her head, prays
as follows:

> Lord, Master, you do not reject women who dedicate them-
> selves to you and who are willing, in a becoming way, to serve
> your Holy House, but admit them to the order of your ministers
> [λειτουργων]. Grant the gift of your Holy Spirit also to this your
> maidservant who wants to dedicate herself to you, and fulfil in
> her the grace of the diaconate [διακονιας], as you have granted
> to Phoebe the grace of your diaconate [διακονιας], whom you
> had called to the work of the ministry [λειτουργιας]. Grant
> her, Lord, that she may persevere without guilt in your Holy

Temple, that she may carefully guard her behavior, especially her modesty and temperance. Moreover, make your maidservant perfect, so that, when she stands before the judgment seat of your Christ, she may obtain the worthy fruit of her excellent conduct, through the mercy and humanity of your Only Son.

After the "Amen," he puts the stole of the diaconate [το διακονικον ʹωραριον] around her neck, under her veil, arranging the two extremities of the stole toward the front.

When the newly ordained has taken part of the sacred body and precious blood, the archbishop hands her the chalice. She accepts it and puts it on the holy table.

Codex Grottaferrata Γβ 1, Crete (1020)

This codex, also known as the Bessarion, was copied in Constantinople itself in about 1020, following the rites "used by the Patriarch." It served a bishop in Cyprus. A priest from Crete by the name of George Varus gave it to Cardinal Julian of St. Sabina in Rome, during the Council of Florence (1438–45). The cardinal donated it to the Catholic Byzantine monastery of St. Nilus in Grottaferrata.[55]

Prayer for the ordination of a deaconess
[ʹευχη ʹεπι χειροτονιαι διακονισσης]

After the sacred offertory, the doors are opened and, before the deacon starts the litany "All Saints," the woman who is to be ordained is *brought forward*. And after he has said the "Divine Grace" with a loud voice, *she* bows her head. *He* imposes his hand on her head, makes the sign of the cross on it three times, and prays:

Holy and Omnipotent Lord, through the birth of your Only Son our God from a Virgin according to the flesh, you have sanctified the female sex. You grant not only to men, but also to women the grace and coming of the Holy Spirit. Please, Lord, look on this your maidservant and dedicate her to the task of your diaconate [της διακονιας], and pour out into her the rich and abundant giving of your Holy Spirit.

Preserve her so that she may always perform her ministry [λειτουργια] with orthodox faith and irreproachable conduct, according to what is pleasing to you. For to you is due all glory and honor.

After the "Amen," *one of the deacons now says the usual prayers.* While this happens, the archbishop, still holding his hand on the head of the ordinand, prays as follows:

Lord, Master, you do not reject women who dedicate themselves to you and who are willing, in a becoming way, to serve your Holy House, but admit them to the order of your ministers [λειτουργων]. Grant the gift of your Holy Spirit also to this your maidservant who wants to dedicate herself to you, and fulfil in her the grace of the diaconate [διακονιας], as you have granted to Phoebe the grace of your diaconate [διακονιας], whom you had called to the work of the ministry [λειτουργιας]. Grant her, Lord, that she may persevere without guilt in your Holy Temple, that she may carefully guard her behavior, especially her modesty and temperance. Moreover, make your maidservant perfect, so that, when she stands before the judgment seat of your Christ, she may obtain the worthy fruit of her excellent conduct, through the mercy and humanity of your Only Son.

After the "Amen," he puts the stole of the diaconate [το διακονικον 'ωραριον] around her neck, under her veil, arranging the two extremities of the stole toward the front.

[The deacon says,] *"Let us complete prayers."*

When the newly ordained has taken part of the sacred body and blood, the archbishop hands her the *sacred* chalice. She accepts it and *does not distribute it to others, but* puts it on the holy table.

Coislin Codex gr. 213, Paris (1027)

This codex, part of the Coislin collection in the National Library in Paris, reflects the liturgical practice of the patriarch of Constantinople. It may have been copied in Constantinople itself and used by a bishop in the Middle East before it became the property of Henri-Charles de Coislin (1665–1732), prince bishop of Metz and chaplain to the king of France. He was a keen collector of manuscripts, who left his treasure to the Abbey of St. Germain-des-Prés. When part of the treasure had been destroyed by fire, the remainder was entrusted to the National Library. The ordination prayers in this codex are strikingly similar to those of the Cairo Codex (see p. 185).[56]

The order for the ordination [ταξις γινομενη 'επι χειροτονιαι] of a deaconess *who must have lived as a chaste virgin and who is, according to present legislation, single, of good bearing, without exaggerated hairdo, and eminent in character to such an extent that she can truly stand up also to men and earn their respect. For such a woman candidate all is performed that is also performed for male deacons, with only a few differences.*

For she is brought forward to the holy table, her head covered in her veil of which the two edges have been removed from the front. And after the "Divine Grace" has been said, she does not bend the knee as the deacon does, but only bows her head. The pontiff signs it three times, and keeping his hand on her head prays as follows:

Holy and Omnipotent Lord, through the birth of your Only Son our God from a Virgin according to the flesh, you have sanctified the female sex. You grant not only to men, but also to women the grace and coming of the Holy Spirit. Please, Lord, look on this your maidservant and dedicate her to the task of your diaconate [της διακονιας], and pour out into her the rich and abundant giving of your Holy Spirit. Preserve her so that she may always perform her ministry [λειτουργια] with orthodox faith and irreproachable conduct, according to what is pleasing to you. For to you is due all glory and honor.

After the "Amen," *while the deacons' intercessions are said as for male deacons,* the pontiff keeping his hand on the head of the woman who is being ordained, prays as follows:

> Lord, Master, you do not reject women who dedicate themselves to you and who are willing, in a becoming way, to serve your Holy House, but admit them to the order of your ministers [λειτουργων]. Grant the gift of your Holy Spirit also to this your maidservant who wants to dedicate herself to you, and fulfil in her the grace of the diaconate [διακονιας], as you have granted to Phoebe the grace of your diaconate [διακονιας], whom you had called to the work of the ministry [λειτουργιας]. Grant her, Lord, that she may persevere without guilt in your Holy Temple, that she may carefully guard her behavior, especially her modesty and temperance. Moreover, make your maidservant perfect, so that, when she stands before the judgment seat of your Christ, she may obtain the worthy fruit of her excellent conduct, through the mercy and humanity of your Only Son.

After the "Amen," he puts the stole of the diaconate [το διακονικον 'ωραριον] around her neck, under her veil, arranging the two extremities of the stole toward the front.

When the newly ordained has taken part of the sacred body and precious blood, the archbishop hands her the chalice. She accepts it and puts it on the holy table.

Bodleian Codex E.5.13 (1132)

This codex was made for the monastery of the Holy Redeemer in Messina, Sicily, and remained in continuous use there until at least the sixteenth century. Richard Rawlinson bought it and bequeathed it to the Bodleian Library in Oxford in 1775. Part of it was copied from a Constantinopolitan model, another part from other, unknown sources.[57]

Prayer for the ordination of a deaconess
[ˈευχη ᾿επι χειροτονιαι διακονισσης]

After the sacred offertory, the doors are opened and, before the deacon starts the litany "Remembering All the Saints," the woman who is to be ordained deacon is brought forward to the bishop and he says the "Divine Grace" with a loud voice. While she bows her head, the bishop imposes his hand on her head, and making the sign of the cross on it three times, he prays this:

> Holy and Omnipotent Lord, through the birth of your Only Son our God from a Virgin according to the flesh, you have sanctified the female sex. You grant not only to men, but also to women the grace and coming of the Holy Spirit. Please, Lord, look on this your maidservant and dedicate her to the task of your diaconate [της διακονιας], and pour out into her the rich and abundant giving of your Holy Spirit. Preserve her so that she may always perform her ministry [λειτουργια] with orthodox faith and irreproachable conduct, according to what is pleasing to you. For to you is due all glory and honor.

After the "Amen," one of the deacons now starts this prayer:

> Let us implore the Lord in peace. For peace from above. For peace in the whole world. For this holy house. For our archbishop, for his priestly ministry, his reward, his endurance, his peace and salvation and the work of his hands. For *so-and-so* [name of the woman] who is to be ordained deaconess and for her salvation let us pray the Lord. That God who loves people grant her a pure and immaculate diaconate, let us pray the Lord. For all the faithful and those who respect God. And the rest.

While this prayer by the deacon is going on, the archbishop, still holding his hand on the head of the woman who is being ordained, prays as follows:

Lord, Master, you do not reject women who dedicate themselves to you and who are willing, in a becoming way, to serve
your Holy House, but admit them to the order of your ministers
[λειτουργων]. Grant the gift of your Holy Spirit also to this your
maidservant who wants to dedicate herself to you, and fulfil in
her the grace of the diaconate [διακονιας], as you have granted
to Phoebe the grace of your diaconate [διακονιας], whom you
had called to the work of the ministry [λειτουργιας]. Grant
her, Lord, that she may persevere without guilt in your Holy
Temple, that she may carefully guard her behavior, especially
her modesty and temperance. Moreover, make your maidservant
perfect, so that, when she stands before the judgment seat of
your Christ, she may obtain the worthy fruit of her excellent
conduct, through the mercy and humanity of your Only Son.

After the "Amen," he puts the stole of the diaconate [το διακονικον
ʹωραριον] around her neck, under her veil, arranging the two extremities of the stole toward the front. *And the deacon who stands in the
ambo says "Remembering All the Saints."*

When she has taken part of the sacred body and precious blood,
the pontiff hands her the chalice. She accepts it and puts it on the
holy table.

Codex Vaticanus gr. 1872 (twelfth century)

*The copy of this codex, now in the Vatican Library in Rome,
was made in either Sicily or in Calabria, southern Italy, possibly
for the bishop of Reggio, capital of Calabria.*[58]

Prayer for the ordination of a deaconess
[ʹευχη ʹεπι χειροτονιαι διακονισσης]

After the sacred offertory, the woman who is to be ordained deacon is
brought forward to the archbishop. And he, calling with a loud voice,
says the "Divine Grace." While she only bows her head, he imposes

his hand on her, makes the sign of the cross on it three times, and prays as follows:

> Holy and Omnipotent Lord, through the birth of your Only Son our God from a Virgin according to the flesh, you have sanctified the female sex. You grant not only to men, but also to women the grace and coming of the Holy Spirit. Please, Lord, look on this your maidservant and dedicate her to the task of your diaconate [της διακονιας], and pour out into her the rich and abundant giving of your Holy Spirit. Preserve her so that she may always perform her ministry [λειτουργια] with orthodox faith and irreproachable conduct, according to what is pleasing to you. For to you is due all glory and honor.

After this the deacon says the diaconal prayers mentioned before.

And the bishop, still holding his hand on the woman who has been ordained, prays as follows:

> Lord, Master, you do not reject women who dedicate them-selves to you and who are willing, in a becoming way, to serve your Holy House, but admit them to the order of your ministers [λειτουργων]. Grant the gift of your Holy Spirit also to this your maidservant who wants to dedicate herself to you, and fulfil in her the grace of the diaconate [διακονιας], as you have granted to Phoebe the grace of your diaconate [διακονιας], whom you had called to the work of the ministry [λειτουργιας]. Grant her, Lord, that she may persevere without guilt in your Holy Temple, that she may carefully guard her behavior, especially her modesty and temperance. Moreover, make your maidservant perfect, so that, when she stands before the judgment seat of your Christ, she may obtain the worthy fruit of her excellent conduct, through the mercy and humanity of your Only Son.

Afterward he puts the stole of the diaconate [το διακονικον 'ωραριον] around her neck, under her veil, arranging the two extremities of the stole toward the front. *Then the deacon who stands in the ambo says "All the Saints."*

When she has received [communion], the priest hands her the *sacred* chalice. She accepts it and *does not distribute it to others, but* puts it on the holy table, *and leaves.*

Cairo Codex gr. 149–104 (fourteenth century)

This codex is found in the library of the Patriarchate of Alexandria. The library itself is very old (third century?), but it suffered enormous losses. After the Arab conquest there was a large gap (642–750), but some manuscripts, such as the famous Codex Alexandrinus (fourth century), were saved. Between 997 and 1928, the library was housed in Cairo. Our codex was a ritual, possibly used by the patriarch of Alexandria himself for some centuries after 1400.[59]

The order for the ordination [ταξις γινομενη ’επι χειροτονιαι] of a deaconess *who must have lived as a chaste virgin and who is, according to present legislation, single, of good bearing, without exaggerated hairdo, and eminent in character to such an extent that she can truly stand up also to men and earn their respect. For such a woman candidate all is performed that is also performed for male deacons, with only a few differences.*

For she is brought forward to the holy table, her head covered in her veil of which the two edges have been removed from the front. And after the "Divine Grace" has been said, she does not bend the knee as the deacon does, but only bows her head. The pontiff signs it three times, and keeping his hand on her head prays as follows, while the deacon says, "Let us pray the Lord":

Holy and Omnipotent Lord, through the birth of your Only Son our God from a Virgin according to the flesh, you have sanctified the female sex. You grant not only to men, but also to women the grace and coming of the Holy Spirit. Please, Lord,

look on this your maidservant and dedicate her to the task of
your diaconate [της διακονιας], and pour out into her the rich
and abundant giving of your Holy Spirit. Preserve her so that she
may always perform her ministry [λειτουργια] with orthodox
faith and irreproachable conduct, according to what is pleasing
to you. For to you is due all glory and honor.

While the deacons' intercessions are said as for male deacons, the
pontiff keeping his hand on the head of the woman who is being
ordained, prays as follows:

Lord, Master, you do not reject women who dedicate themselves to you and who are willing, in a becoming way, to serve
your Holy House, but admit them to the order of your ministers
[λειτουργων]. Grant the gift of your Holy Spirit also to this your
maidservant who wants to dedicate herself to you, and fulfil in
her the grace of the diaconate [διακονιας], as you have granted
to Phoebe the grace of your diaconate [διακονιας], whom you
had called to the work of the ministry [λειτουργιας]. Grant
her, Lord, that she may persevere without guilt in your Holy
Temple, that she may carefully guard her behavior, especially
her modesty and temperance. Moreover, make your maidservant
perfect, so that, when she stands before the judgment seat of
your Christ, she may obtain the worthy fruit of her excellent
conduct, through the mercy and humanity of your Only Son.

After the "Amen," he puts the stole of the diaconate [το διακονικον
ʽωραριον] around her neck, under her veil, arranging the two extremities of the stole toward the front. *Then the deacon who stands in the
ambo says "Remembering All the Saints."*

*When the moment comes for the taking part in the sacred mysteries,
she shares in the divine body and blood after the male deacons. But
when she receives the chalice from the hands of the pontiff, she does
not distribute it but instantly puts it on the holy table. With this the
ordination of the deaconess is completed.*

Xenophon Codex gr. 163 (fourteenth century)

The Monastery of St. Xenophon on Mount Athos was founded in the eleventh century and was destroyed and rebuilt a number of times. It houses a collection of three hundred manuscripts, including this precious eucologion, *which until recently was used for the liturgy in the monastery itself.*[60]

Prayer for the ordination of a deaconess
['ευχη 'επι χειροτονιαι διακονισσης]

After the sacred offertory, the doors are opened and, before the deacon starts the litany "All Saints," the woman who is to be ordained deacon is brought before the pontiff. And after he has said the "Divine Grace" with a loud voice, the woman to be ordained bows her head. He imposes his hand on her forehead, makes the sign of the cross on it three times, and prays:

> Holy and Omnipotent Lord, through the birth of your Only Son our God from a Virgin according to the flesh, you have sanctified the female sex. You grant not only to men, but also to women the grace and coming of the Holy Spirit. Please, Lord, look on this your maidservant and dedicate her to the task of your diaconate [της διακονιας], and pour out into her the rich and abundant giving of your Holy Spirit. Preserve her so that she may always perform her ministry [λειτουργια] with orthodox faith and irreproachable conduct, according to what is pleasing to you. For to you is due all glory and honor.

After the "Amen," one of the deacons now starts this prayer:

> Let us implore the Lord in peace. For peace from above, let us pray the Lord. For peace in the whole world. For this our archbishop, for his priestly ministry, his reward, his endurance, his peace and salvation and the work of his hands, let us pray the Lord. For *so-and-so* [name of the woman] who is to receive the diaconate and for her salvation. That God who loves people

grant her a pure and immaculate diaconate, let us pray the Lord. For our pious emperor who is protected by God, etc., etc.

While the deacon makes these intercessions, the archbishop, still imposing his hand on the head of the ordinand, prays as follows:

Lord, Master, you do not reject women who dedicate themselves to you and who are willing, in a becoming way, to serve your Holy House, but admit them to the order of your ministers [λειτουργων]. Grant the gift of your Holy Spirit also to this your maidservant who wants to dedicate herself to you, and fulfil in her the grace of the diaconate [διακονιας], as you have granted to Phoebe the grace of your diaconate [διακονιας], whom you had called to the work of the ministry [λειτουργιας]. Grant her, Lord, that she may persevere without guilt in your Holy Temple, that she may carefully guard her behavior, especially her modesty and temperance. Moreover, make your maidservant perfect, so that, when she stands before the judgment seat of your Christ, she may obtain the worthy fruit of her excellent conduct, through the mercy and humanity of your Only Son.

After the "Amen," he puts the stole of the diaconate [το διακονικον ὡραριον] around her neck, under her veil, arranging the two extremities of the stole toward the front.

When the newly ordained has taken part of the sacred body and precious blood, the archbishop hands her the chalice. She accepts it and puts it on the holy table.

Notes

1. Enigma at Constantinople

1. The reconstruction of the order of the eucharist follows F. Probst, "Die antiochenische Messe nach den Schriften des heiligen Johannes Chrysostomus dargestellt," *Zeitschrift für katholische Theologie* 7 (1883): 250–303.

2. The original Greek says *diakonous,* using the male noun, not *diakonissas,* the female. This usage of the male noun, which is frequent in early sources, indicates the sameness of their diaconate with that of men.

3. Palladius, Historia ecclesiastica lausiaca, J. P. Migne, *Patrologia graeca,* vol. 47, cols. 56–61; Sozomen, *Historia ecclesiastica* 8:9, Migne, *Patrologia graeca,* vol. 62, col. 1537. St. Olympias is remembered in the Eastern liturgical calendar on July 25, in the West on December 17.

4. K. Ware, "Man, Woman and the Priesthood of Christ," in *Women and the Priesthood,* ed. T. Hopko (New York, 1983), 9–37.

5. P. Zagano, *Holy Saturday: An Argument for the Restoration of the Female Diaconate in the Catholic Church* (New York, 2000).

6. Session XXIII, *On the Sacrament of Ordination,* canon 6. *Enchiridion Symbolorum,* Denzinger-Schönmetzer (Freiburg, 1976), no. 1776.

7. H. Jorissen, "Theologische Bedenken gegen die Diakonatsweihe von Frauen," in *Ein Amt für Frauen in der Kirche — Ein frauengerechtes Amt?* (Ostfildern, 1997), 95.

8. D. Ansorge, "Der Diakonat der Frau: Zum gegenwärtigen Forschungsstand," in *Liturgie und Frauenfrage,* ed. T. Berger and A. Gerhards (St. Odilien, 1990), 60; see also H. Hoping, "Diakonat der Frau ohne Frauenpriestertum?" *Schweizerische Kirchenzeitung* 18 (June 14, 2000).

9. C. M. Wilson, review of *The Canonical Implications of Ordaining Women to the Permanent Diaconate,* by the Canon Law Society of America, *www.ewtn.com,* library, 1995.

10. J. Wijngaards, *The Ordination of Women in the Catholic Church: Unmasking a Cuckoo's Egg Tradition* (London and New York, 2001).

2. The evidence for women deacons

1. The word *cheirotonia* is used here, and it soon became a technical term for ordination.

2. The New Testament avoids the term. Only in Hebrews is Christ compared to the Old Testament high priest.

3. B. Botte, "Secundi meriti munus," *Questions Liturgiques et Paroissiales* 21 (1936): 84–88; P. M. Gy, "La théologie des prières anciennes pour l'ordination des évêques et des prêtres," *Revue des Sciences Philosophiques et Théologiques* 58 (1974): 599–617.

4. C. Baur, *John Chrysostom and His Time,* trans. M. Gonzaga, vol. 1 (Belmont, MA, 1988).

5. More about the theology of ministry in E. J. Kilmartin, "Apostolic Office: Sacrament of Christ," *Theological Studies* 36 (1975): 243–65; E. Schillebeeckx, *Kerkelijk ambt* (Overveen, 1980); M. Richards, *A People of Priests: The Ministry of the Catholic Church* (London, 1995); F. Lobinger, *Like His Brothers and Sisters: Ordaining Community Leaders* (New York, 1998); T. F. O'Meara, *Theology of Ministry* (New York and Mahwah, NJ, 1999).

6. B. Brooten, "Junia ... Outstanding among the Apostles," in *Women Priests,* ed. A. Swidler and L. Swidler (Mahwah, NJ, 1977), 141–44.

7. *Epistolam ad Romanos,* Homilia 31, 2, Migne, *Patrologia graeca,* vol. 60, cols. 669–70.

8. Lemaire, "The Ministries in the New Testament, Recent Research," *Theological Bulletin* 3 (1973): 133–66; E. Carroll, "Women and Ministry," *Theological Studies* 36 (1975): 660–88; M. A. Getty, "God's Fellow Worker and Apostleship," in *Women Priests,* ed. Swidler and Swidler, 176–82.

9. G. Lohfink, "Weibliche Diakone im Neuen Testament," in *Die Frau im Urchristentum,* ed. G. Dautzenberg et al. (Freiburg, 1983), 325–26. Dorothea Reininger provides references to twenty-eight scholars who support this position; *Diakonat der Frau in der einen Kirche* (Ostfildern, 1999), p. 63, note 140.

10. J. Daniélou, *The Ministry of Women in the Early Church* (Leighton Buzzard, U.K., 1974), 14; see also N. Brox, *Die Pastoralbriefe* (Regensburg, 1969), 154.

11. H. Frohnhofen, "Weibliche Diakone in der frühen Kirche," *Studien der Zeit* 204 (1986): 269–78; L. Oberlinner, *Kommentar zum ersten Timotheusbrief* (Freiburg, 1994), 139–42; and many others.

12. *Epistolarum Liber* 10, 96, n. 8; M. Durry, *Pline le Jeune,* vol. 4 (Paris, 1947), 74.

13. *Stromata* 3, 6, §53; R. Gryson, *The Ministry of Women in the Early Church* (Collegeville, MN, 1976); originally *Le ministère des femmes dans l'Église ancienne* (Gembloux, 1972), 58.

14. *Commentary on Romans 10:17*; Migne, *Patrologia graeca*, vol. 14, col. 1278.

15. See also 1 Corinthians 12:28–29; *Didache* 10:7.

16. Ignatius, *Smyrnaeans* §13.

17. J. G. Davies, "Deacons, Deaconesses and Minor Orders in the Patristic Period," *Journal of Ecclesiastical History* 14 (1963): 1–23.

3. The manuscripts that preserved the rite

1. Ansorge, "Der Diakonat der Frau," 105; M.-J. Aubert, *Des femmes diacres: Un nouveau chemin pour l'Église* (Paris, 1987) 105; C. Böttigheimer, "Der Diakonat der Frau," *Münchener Theologische Zeitschrift* 47 (1996): 259; Y. Congar, "Gutachten zum Diakonat der Frau," Amtliche Mitteilungen der Gemeinsamen Synode der Bistümer der Bundesrepublik Deutschlands, Munich, 1973, p. 37; H. Frohnhofen, "Weibliche Diakone in der frühen Kirche," *Studien der Zeit* 204 (1986): 276; Gryson, *The Ministry of Women*, 117–18; P. Hofrichter, "Diakonat und Frauen im kirchlichen Amt," *Heiliger Dienst* 50, no. 3 (1996): 152–54; P. Hünermann, "Theologische Argumente für die Diakonatsweihe von Frauen," in *Diakonat: Ein Amt für Frauen in der Kirche — Ein frauengerechtes Amt?* (Ostfildern, 1997), 104; A. Jensen, "Das Amt der Diakonin in der kirchlichen Tradition der ersten Jahrtausend," in *Diakonat: Ein Amt für Frauen in der Kirche — Ein frauengerechtes Amt?* (Ostfildern, 1997), 47; D. Reininger, *Diakonat der Frau in der einen Kirche* (Ostfildern, 1999), 97–98; A. Thiermeyer, "Der Diakonat der Frau," *Theologisch Quartalschrift* 173, no. 3 (1993): 230–31; C. Vagaggini, "L'Ordinazione delle diaconesse nella tradizione greca e bizantina," *Orientalia Christiana Periodica* 40 (1974): 169–73.

2. Vatican Library, ms. Barberini gr. 336, ff. 169r–171v; S. Parenti and E. Velkovska, *L'Eucologio Barberini gr. 336* (Rome, 2000), pp. 170–74 and 336–39.

3. M. Arranz, *L'Eucologio Constantinopolitano agli inizi del secolo XI* (Rome, 1996), 153–60.

4. A. Dmitrievskij, *Opisanie liturgiteskich rukopisej* (Kiev, 1901), 2: 16.

5. R. Devreesse, *Le fonds Coislin* (Paris, 1945), Catalogue des manuscrits grecs, 2, pp. 194–95.

6. A. Jacob, "Un euchologe du Saint-Sauveur 'in lingua Phari' de Messine, le Bodleianus auct. E.5.13," *Bulletin de l'Institut historique belge* (1980): 283–364.

7. J. Morin, *Commentarius* [*sic*] *de sacris ecclesiae ordinationibus* (Antwerp, 1695), 78–81.

8. G. Mercati, "Eucologio di S. Maria del Patire," *Revue Bénédictin* 46 (1934): 233–34.

9. I. Sakkeliôn and A. Sakkeliôn, *Katalogos tôn cheirographôn tês ethnikês bibliothêkês... En Athenais*, 1892, p. 123.

10. Dmitrievskij, *Opisanie*, 3:346–47.

11. Dmitrievskij, *Opisanie*, 2:361.

12. The Byzantine rite was practiced in parts of central Italy until the end of the sixteenth century, and in our own days it is still celebrated by the Italian Byzantine monastery of Grottaferrata in the vicinity of Rome.

13. Morin, *Commentarius*, 52.

14. *Folium* 336. For the words in English, see p. 46. The whole rite covers twelve such sheets.

15. Morin, *Commentarius*, 52.

16. Parenti and Velkovska, *L'Eucologio Barberini*, 19–23.

17. Translation of all three texts my own, based on the original Greek.

4. The rite of ordaining a woman deacon

1. *Lumen gentium* §29.

2. "Prayer at the Ordination of a Deaconess"; Arranz, *L'Eucologio Constantinopolitano*, 153–60.

3. See Vatican Manuscript 1872; Morin, *Commentarius*, 78–81.

4. Evangelos Theodorou, "Die Weihe, die Segnung der Diakoninnen" (in modern Greek), *Theologia* 25 (1954): 430–69; "Das Amt der Diakoninnen in der kirchlichen Tradition: Ein orthodoxer Beitrag zum Problem der Frauenordination," *Una Sancta* 33 (1978): 162–72.

5. Other symbolic elements of ordination have also been considered essential in various eras and regions of Christian tradition, but even then the laying-on of hands and the invocation of the Spirit were admitted to be central.

6. Jacob Goar, in *Euchologion sive rituale graecorum* (Paris, 1647), 262–64; with notes on pp. 264–67.

7. Devreesse, *Le fonds Coislin*, 194–95.

8. The Council of Trent, *On the Sacrament of Ordination*, Canon 4, Denzinger no. 964.

5. The ritual for men and women compared

1. Goar, *Euchologion,* pp. 262–64.
2. Frohnhofen, "Weibliche Diakone." See also Aubert, *Femmes diacres,* 171–90.
3. Kallistos Ware's books are frequently reprinted. *The Orthodox Church* has been republished by Penguin Books (New York, 1993). In 1999, St. Vladimir's Seminary Press (Crestwood, NY) published the collected works of Kallistos Ware in four volumes under the title *The Inner Kingdom.*
4. Kallistos of Diokleia [K. Ware], "Man, Woman and the Priesthood of Christ," in *Women and the Priesthood,* ed. T. Hopko (New York, 1982, reprinted 1999), 16.
5. Teva Regule, "An Interview with Bishop Kallistos Ware," *St. Nina Quarterly* (June 1997).
6. A.-G. Martimort, *Deaconesses: An Historical Study* (San Francisco, 1986), 156.

6. Is talk of "sacrament" an anachronism?

1. Martimort, *Deaconesses,* p. 75, note 66.
2. J. Wijngaards, "When Women Were Deacons," *The Tablet,* May 8, 1999, 623–24.
3. See Hugh of St. Victor, *De Sacramentis* I 9, 7; II, 9, 1–3; Peter Lombard, *Liber Sententiarum,* IV 6, 7. For the distinction between a "sacrament" and a "sacramental," see p. 57.
4. H. Vorgrimler, "Gutachten über die Diakonatsweihe für Frauen," *Synode* (1973), 39–40; B. Weiss, "Zum Diakonat der Frau," *Trierer Theologischer Zeitschrift* 84 (1975): 20; D. Ansorge, "Die wesentlichen Argumente liegen auf dem Tisch: Zur neueren Diskussion um den Diakonat der Frau," *Herder Korrespondenz* 47 (1993): 583.
5. A readable and up-to-date introduction to the sacraments can be found in R. P. McBrien, *Catholicism* (Minneapolis and London, 1980), 2:731–45.
6. *Summa theologiae* III, qq. 60–65.
7. The expression used was *ex opere operato* — "by the working of the deed itself." Trent, Session VII, canons about the sacraments; Denz. 1601–13. This expression was misunderstood by later theologians who wrongly ascribed almost quasi-magical powers to the sacraments.
8. Denz. 1774.

9. B. J. Hilberath, "Das Amt der Diakonin: Ein sakramentales Amt?" in *Diakonat: Ein Amt für Frauen in der Kirche — Ein frauengerechtes Amt?* (Ostfildern, 1997), 218 (my own translation).

10. *Verbum et elementum:* "Take away the word and what can water do? When the word joins the material substance, it becomes a sacrament"; Treatise on St. John 80:3; Migne, *Patrologia latina*, vol. 35, col. 1840.

11. Ambrose, *De Spiritu Sancto* 1, 3, 39–45, Migne, *Patrologia latina*, vol. 16, cols. 742–43; Basil, *De Spiritu Sancto* 12, 28, Migne, *Patrologia graeca*, vol. 2, col. 116.

12. Pope Leo XIII, *Apostolicae curae*, September 18, 1896; *Acta Sanctae Sedis* 29 (1896/97), pp. 198ff.; Denz. 3315–19. In the view of later studies by Church historians and ecumenical relations with the Church of England, it is not certain whether this view is still retained by the Vatican.

13. M. Noth, "Das alttestamentliche Bundesschliessen im Lichte eines Mari-textes," *Gesammelte Studie* (Munich, 1957), 142–54.

14. *The Heavenly Hierarchy* 5, 1, 3; Migne, *Patrologia graeca*, vol. 3, col. 504C.

15. P. Hünermann, "Stellungnahme zu den Anmerkungen von Professor Otto Semmelroth SJ betreffend Votum der Synode zum Weihediakonat der Frau," *Diaconia Christi* 10, no. 1 (1975): 33–38.

16. A. C. Lochmann, *Studien zum Diakonat der Frau* (Siegen, 1996), 167, 189–90.

7. Excluded from "any sacred service"?

1. Martimort, *Deaconesses*, 244.

2. Martimort, *Deaconesses*, 155–56.

3. Martimort, *Deaconesses*, 245.

4. Martimort, *Deaconesses*, 156.

5. *Heptateuch* I §153; *Sermon on Mount* I §34.

6. *Panarion* 79 §1.

7. Tertullian, *Veiling of Virgins* c. 10; Ambrosiaster, *On 1 Cor. 14:34*.

8. *Homily* 37 §1.

9. *Apost. Constit.* III §9, 1–4.

10. *Apost. Constit.* VII §27; see texts on p. 160.

11. F. R. McManus, "Book Review: Deaconesses: An Historical Study," *The Jurist* 47 (1987): 597.

12. *Canons of the Council of Nicea,* Can. 4; *Ante-Nicene Fathers,* series 2, vol. 14.

13. Decretum Gratiani, *Corpus juris canonici*, ed. A. Friedberg (Leipzig, 1879–81; reprint Graz, 1955); Dist. 23, c. 25=vol. 1, col. 85; Sect III, Dist.

1 de cons., c. 41=vol. 1, col. 1304–5; Sect III, Dist. 1 de cons., c. 42.=vol. 1, col. 1305.

14. K. K. FitzGerald, *Women Deacons in the Orthodox Church* (Brookline, MA, 1998), 79.

15. P. F. Bradshaw, *Ordination Rites of the Ancient Churches of East and West* (New York, 1990), 88; E. Theodorou, *The "Ordination"* [χειροτονια] or *"Appointment"* [χειροθεσια] *of Women Deacons* (Athens, 1954), 62–63.

16. I. M. Vosté, *Pontificale iuxta ritum Syrorum orientalium, id est, Chaldaeorum, Versio latina* (Vatican, 1937/38), 158–61. As to Pseudo-Dionysius "not allowing women deacons to genuflect," he does not mention women deacons in his comment on the difference between priests and deacons.

17. *On 1 Tim. 3:11*. For the full text, see p. 163.

18. Vagaggini, "L'Ordinazione delle diaconesse," 181–82; A. Thiermeyer, "Diakonat der Frau," 233.

19. Vagaggini, "L'Ordinazione delle diaconesse," 185; Thiermeyer, "Diakonat der Frau," 234. Nestorian and Monophysite sources of the fifth and sixth centuries record that women deacons, in certain circumstances, served at the altar and distributed holy communion to women and children.

20. *Testamentum Domini* II 20, 7.

8. Just a minor role at baptism?

1. Martimort, *Deaconesses*, 43.

2. Martimort, *Deaconesses*, 131–32.

3. Martimort, *Deaconesses*, 134.

4. A. Piédagnel, ed., *Catéchèse mystagogique* (Paris, 1966), 108–9; J. Wenger, *Jean Chrysostome: Huit catéchèses baptismales inédites* (Paris, 1957), 93.

5. *Catechetical Sermon* 14, 8.

6. Wenger, *Jean Chrysostome*, 147.

7. Novella 6, §3; see the full text on Texts, p. 170.

8. *Didascalia* 16 §2–3; see full text on p. 152. In the Latin, which is the only version available for this text, the term *diaconissa* appears, but Roger Gryson has shown, from comparisons with parallel passages in the *Apostolic Constitutions*, that the original Greek had the female 'η διακονος, γυνη διακονος; *Ministry*, p. 138, note 61.

9. P. F. Bradshaw, ed., *Essays in Early Eastern Initiation* (Bramcote, U.K., 1988); T. M. Finn, *Early Christian Baptism and the Catechumenate* (Collegeville, MN, 1992); E. Ferguson, ed., *Conversion, Catechumenate, and Baptism in the Early Church* (New York, 1993); M. E. Johnson, ed.,

Living Water, Sealing Spirit: Readings on Christian Initiation (Collegeville, MN, 1995; T. M. Finn, *From Death to Rebirth: Ritual and Conversion in Antiquity* (New York, 1997); J. Day, *Baptism in Early Byzantine Palestine, 325–451* (Cambridge, 1999); M. E. Johnson, *The Rites of Christian Initiation: Their Evolution and Interpretation* (Collegeville, MN, 1999).

10. Ancient rule in the *Statuta ecclesiae antiqua,* chapter 12. Deaconesses had ceased to exist in the West at the time of the Statuta's redaction, so "widows or nuns" was substituted for "deaconesses" in the text.

11. *Ecclesiastical Canons of the Holy Apostles,* can. 19.

12. An ancient Coptic ritual from Egypt; H. Denzinger, *Ritus Orientalium* (Würzburg, 1863), 1:192–214; Ritual of Jacob of Edessa, 279–88; see also Theodore of Mopsuestia, John Chrysostom, Cyril of Jerusalem, etc.

13. *Apostolic Constitutions* 3, 15 (fourth century); the text is an adaptation of *Didascalia* 16 §2–3, and not entirely clear in its details.

14. *Ordo baptismi* of Ishô'yabh III; G. Dietrich, *Die nestorianische Taufliturgie ins Deutsche übersetzt und unter Verwertung der neuesten handschriftlichen Funde historisch-kritisch erforscht* (Giessen, 1903), 96–99.

15. *Didascalia* 16 §3; see full text on p. 152.

16. In their section on widows, the *Didascalia* (3.9.1) and the *Apostolic Constitutions* (3.9.1) both state that it is not advisable for one woman to baptize another woman, since it is "a big risk for the women who undertake this." This either reflects the fact that these pastoral collections were compiled from conflicting sources, or it condemns a practice that excluded the proper ministers: the priest and the woman deacon; F. X. Funk, *Didascalia et constitutiones apostolorum* (Paderborn, 1905), 1:198–99.

17. In the Syriac *Testamentum Domini* 2, 8 (AD 475) we read: "The women who are to be baptized should be anointed by the widows who have precedence [= ordained widows], while the priest says the words over them. Similarly, during the baptism itself, the same widows should hold the women inside a veil, putting the veil before them while the bishop speaks the formula of the profession [of faith], and also when he speaks the formula of renunciation"; I. E. Rahmani, *Testamentum Domini nostri Jesu Christi* (Munich, 1899), 129–31. Another Syriac text of later date, the *Book of the Fathers* (thirteenth–fourteenth centuries), preserves a similar tradition. "Deaconesses perform the sacrament of baptism for women because it is not right for the priest to see the nakedness of women. That is why the deaconesses anoint the women and baptize them in water. The priest should stretch his hand through a window or through a veil to sign the candidates, while the deaconess should perform both the anointing and the baptism

itself"; I. M. Vosté, *Liber Patrum,* codificazione canonica orientale, fonti, ser. 2, no. 16 (Vatican, 1940), 34.

18. *Didascalia* 16 §4; see full text on p. 152.

19. It is likely that originally the newly baptized were anointed with chrism over the whole body. This can be derived from the symbolism and from the fact that in most rites chrism was applied, not only to the forehead but also to the nostrils, the eyes, the lips, the ears, the hands, the feet, the breast, and between the shoulders.

20. John Chrysostom, *Catechesis ad Ilium.* 2 §27; *Sources chrétiennes* no. 50 (Paris), 148–49.

21. F. C. Conybeare and O. Wardrop, "The Georgian Version of the Liturgy of St. James," *Revue de l'Orient chrétien* 19 (1914): 23–33.

9. No anointing of the sick?

1. Martimort, *Deaconesses,* 247.

2. General introductions: C. W. Gusmer, *The Ministry of Healing in the Church of England: An Ecumenical-Liturgical Study* (Great Wakering, U.K., 1974); J. L. Empereur, *Prophetic Anointing: God's Call to the Sick, the Elderly, and the Dying* (Wilmington, 1982); C. W. Gusmer, *And You Visited Me: Sacramental Ministry to the Sick and the Dying* (New York, 1984); P. E. Fink, *Anointing the Sick* (Collegeville, MN, 1987); J. J. Ziegler, *Let Them Anoint the Sick* (Collegeville, MN, 1987); A. J. Cuschieri, *Anointing of the Sick: A Theological and Canonical Study* (Lanham, MD, 1993). Historical reconstructions can be found in J. Dauvillier, "Extrême Onction dans les Eglises orientales," *Dictionnaire de Droit Canonique,* vol. 5 (1953), 725–89; M. T. Kelsey, *Healing and Christianity: In Ancient Thought and Modern Times* (New York, 1973); M. Dudley and G. Rowell, eds., *The Oil of Gladness: Anointing in the Christian Tradition* (Collegeville, MN, 1993).

3. *Demonstration* 23 §3; Graffin, *Patrologia syriaca,* 1:55.

4. Dauvillier, "Extrême Onction," 731–33.

5. Goar, *Euchologion,* 417.

6. *De Extreme Unctione,* Sess. 14, ch. 3 and can. 4; Denzinger, nos. 1697–99, 1719.

7. *Letter to Decentius,* bishop of Giobbe in Italy; Migne, *Patrologia latina,* vol. 20, cols. 559ff.

8. Dauvillier, "Extrême Onction," 780.

9. *Against Heresies* c. 79; see p. 154.

10. *Novella* 6 §3; see p. 170.

11. *Didascalia* 16 §5; see p. 152.

12. *Apostolic Constitutions* III, no. 15.

13. Commentary on 1 Corinthians; see p. 148.

14. Cornelius Nepos (100–25 BC); *The Book on the Great Generals of Foreign Nations,* trans. J. C. Rolfe (Cambridge, MA, 1947), 371.

15. Innocent I (416), *Letter to Decentius,* bishop of Giobbe in Italy; Migne, *Patrologia latina,* vol. 20, cols. 559ff.; Theodulf, bishop of Orleans (AD 789), *Capitulare* 2, Migne, *Patrologia latina,* vol. 105, cols. 220–21.

16. Canon 28; E. Tidner, *Didascalia apostolorum canonum ecclesiasti-corum* (Berlin, 1963), 110–12.

17. Book II, 20 §7; I. E. Rahmani, *Testamentum Domini nostri Jesu Christi* (Munich, 1899), 142–43.

18. "She visits and anoints women who are ill"; Syriac Pontifical of Michael the Great (AD 1172), I. M. Vosté, *Pontificale iuxta ritum Eccle-siae occidentalium* (Rome, 1941–44), 201–2. "She anointed women when they were sick"; Bar Hebraeus (1225–86), cf. W. de Vries, *Sakramenten-theologie bei den syrischen Monophysiten* (Rome, 1940), 220. "They anoint the naked bodies of women both at baptism and confirmation, and at ex-treme unction"; Maronite Synod of Mount Lebanon (AD 1736), I. D. Mansi, ed., *Sacrorum conciliorum nova et amplissima collectio* (Paris, 1907), cols. 163–64. Though these are relatively late sources, they belong to the same Byzantine area in which we find the Greek tradition, and thus may preserve traces of the past.

19. *On the Life on St. Macrina;* Migne, *Patrologia latina,* vol. 46, col. 992. Following E. Theodorou, K. K. FitzGerald interprets this as referring to Macrina's service at the altar. I believe it refers more naturally to Ma-crina's sacramental ministry to dying women; K. K. FitzGerald, *Women Deacons,* 117.

20. S. Maffei, *Museum Veronense* (Verona, 1749), 179.

21. See, for instance, Codex Sinai gr. 973 (AD 1153). B. J. Groen, *Ter Genezing van Ziel en Lichaam* (Nijmegen, 1991), 23.

22. *Didascalia* 16 §5; see p. 152.

23. See also after Jesus' death: Mark 16:1; Luke 23:56; E. Carroll, "Women and Ministry," *Theological Studies* 36 (1975): 667.

24. J. Daniélou, *The Ministry of Women in the Early Church* (Leighton Buzzard, U.K., 1974; originally in *Maison Dieu,* no. 61 [1960]: 29); Vagaggini, "L'Ordinazione delle diaconesse," 189.

10. Merely nuns, and not true deacons?

1. Martimort, *Deaconesses,* 155.

2. Martimort, *Deaconesses,* 156.

3. Martimort, *Deaconesses*, 242–43.

4. Monophysites (literally: one-nature believers) thought that Christ's divine person took over his human nature so that no human nature remained in Christ.

5. Letter 62; E. W. Brooks, *The Sixth Book of the Selected Letters of Severus* (London, 1903), 2:193–94.

6. *Novella* 3 §1.

7. *Novella* 123 §30 (decree of AD 546).

8. *Novella* 6 §3–5; see p. 170.

9. *Novella* 6 §8 and 10; see p. 171.

10. FitzGerald, *Women Deacons*, 90.

11. U. E. Eisen, *Amtsträgerinnen im frühen Christentum* (Göttingen, 1996), 154–57.

12. G. H. R. Horsley, *New Documents Illustrating Early Christianity* (North Ryde, U.K., 1987) 4:240–41.

13. Martimort, *Deaconesses*, 154.

14. Canons 22 and 23; C. J. Hefele and H. Leclercq, *Histoire des conciles d'après les documents originaux*, vol. 1/2 (Paris, 1907), 1012.

15. Ανδρες και γυναικες διακονοι; *Novella* 3, prol.; 3, 1, 1; 3, 2, 1; 6, tit.; etc.; Gryson, *Ministry of Women*, 72.

11. Only a rare and local phenomenon?

1. Johannes Moschus, *Pratum Spirituale* ch. 3; Migne, *Patrologia graeca*, vol. 87, col. 2853; see also Martimort, *Deaconesses*, 132–33; Gryson, *Ministry of Women*, 150, note 280.

2. Eisen, *Amtsträgerinnen*, 160–63.

3. Eisen, *Amtsträgerinnen*, 154–60.

4. The main sources are the *Meterikon*, compiled around 1200, ed. D. Tsamis (Thessaloniki, 1990), vols. 1–3, and the *Megas Synaxaristes*, ed. V. Matheou (Attica, 1956).

5. More information about women deacon saints in FitzGerald, *Women Deacons*, 201.

6. Eisen, *Amtsträgerinnen*, 163–65. "Footwashing" had many meanings in the Early Church. Could there be a reference here to her ministry at baptism? See B. Kötting, "Fußwaschung," *Reallexikon für Antike und Christentum*, vol. 8 (Stuttgart, 1957), cols. 743–77; J. C. Thomas, *Footwashing in John 13 and the Johannine Community* (Sheffield, 1991).

7. Eisen, *Amtsträgerinnen*, 182–83.

8. Eisen, *Amtsträgerinnen*, 175–77.

9. *Novella* 3,1 of Justinian; there were one hundred male deacons.

10. Wijngaards, *Ordination of Women.*

11. Synod of Orange (441), can. 26: "Altogether no [more] women deacons are to be ordained. If some already exist, let them bend their heads to the blessing given to the (lay) people"; the Synod of Epaon (517), can. 21.

12. *Response to the interrogations of Mark* §35; Migne, *Patrologia graeca,* vol. 138, col. 988; Martimort, *Deaconesses,* 172.

13. *Scholion on the Council of Chalcedon;* Migne, *Patrologia graeca,* vol. 137, col. 441; Martimort, *Deaconesses,* 171. Balsamon was wrong on women deacons' access to the altar, as we have seen in chapter 7.

14. Bishop Kallistos Ware; see "An Interview with Bishop Kallistos Ware," by Teva Regule, *St. Nina Quarterly,* June 1997.

15. See the texts listed on pp. 167–68, 169–72, 174.

12. Did the bishops not intend to ordain real deacons?

1. In the Greek-speaking world, χειροτονια, as opposed to χειροθεσια, acquired its restrictive, sacramental meaning only from about the eighth century.

2. See chapter 6 for a discussion of the terminology. Experts speak of the *determinatio ex adjunctis,* the determination of the sign by ceremonies that are joined to it.

3. Martimort, *Deaconesses,* 152–53, esp. note 32.

4. *In Epistolas,* 132–34.

5. *About sacred ordinations,* ch. 156; Migne, *Patrologia graeca,* vol. 155, cols. 361–3; see also chapters 241–45; cols. 461–63; cf. C. Skouteris, *La place de l'ordination dans la théologie sacramentaire de Jean de Thessalonique* (Strasbourg, 1969), 32–35.

6. E. Theodorou, *The "Ordination"* [χειροτονια] *or "Appointment"* [χειροθεσια] *of Women Deacons* (Athens, 1954), 583.

7. *Apostolic Constitutions* VIII, 17–20; see p. 161.

8. *Letter 146 to the priest Evangelos; Corpus scriptorum ecclesiasticorum latinorum* (Vienna, 1866), 56:310.

9. C. Vogel, "Chirotonie et Chirothésie: Importance et relativité du geste de l'imposition des mains dans la collation des ordres," *Irénikon* 45 (1972): 7–21.

10. Martimort, *Deaconesses,* 153.

11. "Divine grace of the most holy Spirit be with you, enlightening you, confirming you, and making you intelligent all the days of your life." Cf. ⁻in, *Commentarius,* 96. This is *not* the classic proclamation.

12. "For such a woman candidate all is performed that is also performed for male deacons, with only a few [i.e., the following] differences"; Coislin Codex and Cairo Codex, see pp. 180, 185.

13. *Ecclesiastical Hierarchy,* 5, 5; Migne, *Patrologia graeca,* vol. 3, col. 512.

14. *On the Priesthood,* 4, 1; Migne, *Patrologia graeca,* vol. 48, col. 662.

15. *Oration* 18, 35; Migne, *Patrologia graeca,* vol. 35, col. 1032.

16. "La formule d'ordination 'La Grace Divine' dans les rites orientaux," *L'Orient Syrien* 2 (1957): 286–96.

17. R. Sohm, *Kirchenrecht* (Munich, 1923), 2:263.

18. Theodoret of Cyrrhus (393–458), *History of the Church,* V 12,1; about all this see the excellent article by Pierre-Marie Gy, "Les anciennes prières d'ordination," *La Maison–Dieu* 138 (1979): 93–122.

19. Ordination prayer in the *Apostolic Constitutions*; see p. 161.

20. First ordination prayer in the standard rite; see pp. 175–188.

21. Second ordination prayer in the standard rite; see pp. 175–188.

22. J. D. Zizioulas, *Priesteramt und Priesterweihe im Licht der östlich — orthodoxen Theologie* (Freiburg, 1973); J. Erickson, "The Priesthood in Patristic Teaching," in *The Place of the Woman in the Orthodox Church and the Question of the Ordination of Women,* ed. G. Limouris (Katerini, Greece, 1992), pp. 108–9; FitzGerald, *Women Deacons,* 106.

23. Gy, "Anciennes prières," esp. 112–14.

24. Martimort, *Deaconesses,* 154–55.

25. Gy, "Anciennes prières," esp. 110–11; see also M. Hanssens, "Les oraisons sacramentelles des ordinations orientales," in *La liturgie d'Hippolyte* (Rome, 1970), 2:263–85; G. Kretschmar, "Probleme des orthodoxen Amtsverständnisses," in *Das Amt im ökomenischen Kontext,* ed. J. Baur (Stuttgart, 1980), 9–32.

13. Tackling the underlying assumptions

1. Hofrichter, "Diakonat und Frauen," 152.

2. F. R. McManus, "Book Review: Diaconesses: An Historical Study," *The Jurist* 47 (1987): 597.

3. McManus, "Book Review," 597.

4. Martimort, "La question du service des femmes à l'autel," *Notitiae* 16 (1980): 8–16.

5. Martimort, "La question," 12; cf. P. Hünermann, "Theologische Argumente," 109–11.

6. Martimort, *Deaconesses,* 172, 245 and passim.

7. Read, for instance, the letter of Fr. Calmette of January 24, 1733; *Lettres édifiantes et curieuses* (Paris, 1910), 7:503–5.

8. G. Müller, *Priesthood and Diaconate* (San Francisco, 2002), 219–20.

9. *Summa theologiae* I qu. 92 art. 1 ad 1.

10. *Summa theologiae* II qu. 18 art. 1.

11. *Summa theologiae* II qu. 18 art. 1 ad 3.

12. *Summa theologiae* I qu. 92 art. 1.

13. *Summa theologiae* I qu. 92 art. 1 ad 2.

14. *Summa theologiae* I qu. 92 art. 2.

15. *Summa theologiae* I qu. 93 art. 4 ad 1.

16. *Summa theologiae suppl.* qu. 39 art. 1.

17. *Summa theologiae suppl.* qu. 39 art. 1.

18. Gerhard Müller, "Kann nur der getaufte Mann gültig das Weihesakrament empfangen?" in *Frauen in der Kirche* (Würzburg, 1999), 328.

19. Read his totally inadequate discussion of Dorothea Reininger's 736-page monumental work on the diaconate of women, *Diakonat der Frau in der Einen Kirche* (Ostfildern, 1999). See Müller, *Priesthood and Diaconate,* 43–52. Müller responds to Reininger's facts with a theological "it cannot be so."

20. Müller, *Priesthood and Diaconate,* 48.

21. For instance, the Second Synod of Tours in Gaul, AD 567.

22. Müller, *Priesthood and Diaconate,* 48.

23. Martimort, *Deaconesses,* 156.

24. Müller, *Priesthood and Diaconate,* 154.

25. Interview with Gerhard Ludwig Müller, "Das dreistufige Weiheamt muss eine Einheit bleiben," *Die Tagespost,* December 11, 2001, 5–6; my translation.

26. Interview with Gerhard Ludwig Müller.

27. John Wijngaards, *Did Christ Rule Out Women Priests?* (Great Wakering, U.K.: McCrimmons, 1977, 1986).

28. John Wijngaards, *The Ordination of Women in the Catholic Church: Unmasking a Cuckoo's Egg Tradition* (London and New York, 2001).

29. *Didascalia* 16 §1; see full text in Texts p. 151.

14. How certain are our conclusions?

1. The principle was clearly laid down by the Council of Florence (De-^cor the Armenians; AD 1439) and by the Council of Trent (session 7,

can. 11; AD 1547); Denzinger 1955, nos 695 and 854 [= old Denz. 695 and 854].

2. Denzinger 1955, no. 297 [= old Denz. 297].

3. Leo XIII on Anglican Ordination, September 13, 1896, *Collectanea de Propaganda Fide* (Rome, 1954), 345. Read the full discussion on certainty regarding the minister's intention in M. Prümmer, *Manuale Theologiae Moralis* (Freiburg, 1936), 3:50–57.

4. Prümmer, *Manuale*, 1:6. Italics added.

5. *Dei Verbum* §8; W. M. Abbott, ed., *The Documents of Vatican II* (New York, 1966), 116.

6. Kallistos of Diokleia [K. Ware], "Man, Woman and the Priesthood of Christ," in *Women and the Priesthood*, ed. T. Hopko (New York, 1982, reprinted 1999), 16.

7. E. Theodorou, "The Institution of Deaconesses in the Orthodox Church and the Possibility of Its Restoration," in *The Place of the Woman in the Orthodox Church and the Question of the Ordination of Women*, ed. G. Limouris (Katerini, Greece, 1992), 212–13.

8. Gryson, *Ministry of Women*, 120.

9. Vagaggini, "L'Ordinazione delle diaconesse," 188.

10. P. Hünermann, "Conclusions regarding the Female Diaconate," *Theological Studies* 36 (1975): 327–28.

11. Thiermeyer, "Diakonat der Frau," 233–34.

12. Hofrichter, "Diakonat und Frauen," 152–54.

13. Jensen, "Das Amt," 49.

14. Ansorge, "Diakonat der Frau," 46–47.

15. Böttigheimer, "Diakonat der Frau," 261–62.

16. FitzGerald, *Women Deacons*, 120–21.

17. Zagano, *Holy Saturday*, 98–102.

18. Reininger, *Diakonat der Frau*, 126.

19. Congar, "Gutachten zum Diakonat," 37–41.

20. J. La Porte, *The Role of Women in Early Christianity* (Toronto, 1982), esp. 112–19.

21. H. Frohnhofen, "Weibliche Diakone," 276.

22. Aubert, *Femmes diacres*, 105.

23. A. C. Lochmann, *Studien zum Diakonat der Frau* (Siegen, 1996), esp. 177ff.

24. P. Luislampe, "Diakonat der Frau?" in *Diakonat der Frau — Chance für dei Zukunft?* (Münster, 1996), 23–36.

25. A. Swidler, "Women Deacons: Historical Highlights," in *A New Phoebe: Perspectives on Roman Catholic Women and the Permanent*

Diaconate, ed. A. Swidler and V. Ratigan (Kansas City, MO, 1990), 81–88.

26. N. Reynolds et al. for the Canon Law Society of America, *The Canonical Implications of Ordaining Women to the Permanent Diaconate* (Washington, DC, 1995), esp. 18–21.

27. C. R. Meyer, "Ordained Women in the Early Church," *Chicago Studies* 4 (1965): 285–308.

28. E. Behr-Sigel, "Ordination von Frauen?" in *Warum keine Ordination der Frau?* ed. E. Gössmann and D. Bader (Munich, 1987), 50–72.

29. V. Karras, "Women in the Eastern Church; Past, Present and Future," *Voithia,* December 15, 1997.

30. Div. 25, art. 2. q. 1; *Commentarium in IV libros sententiarum magistri Petri Lombardi* by Bonaventure, 1251–53; published in *Opera Omnia,* Quaracchi 1882–1902, 4:649.

15. Facing up to the past, for the sake of the future

1. The official Vatican documents limit themselves to affirming that no women were ordained *priests. Inter insigniores,* October 15, 1976, §5–8; "Declaration of the Sacred Congregation for the Doctrine of the Faith on the Question of the Admission of Women to the Ministerial Priesthood," *Briefing* 7 (1977), nos. 5–6; "Official Commentary by the Congregation," *L'Osservatore Romano,* January 27, 1977; *Ordinatio sacerdotalis,* May 22, 1994, "Apostolic Letter by Pope John Paul II on Reserving Priestly Ordination to Men Alone," *Origins* 24 (June 9, 1994).

2. Holy Office condemnation, February 13, 1633.

3. Letter to Duchess Christina von Lotharingen, 1615, in *Briefe zur Weltgeschichte,* ed. K. H. Peter (Munich, 1964), 80–82.

4. Καταστάθησα, the same word for ordination also used in the *Didascalia.*

5. H. Leclercq, *Dictionnaire d'archéologie chrétienne* (Paris, 1921), vol. 4, cols. 570–71.

6. London: Darton, Longman & Todd, 2001; New York: Continuum, 2001, chapters 8 to 15.

7. J. P. Mackey, *The Christian Experience of God as Trinity* (London, 1983), 135–37. About the inclusion of the Spirit as a separate "Person," see also the divergent views of A. W. Wainwright, *The Trinity in the New Testament* (London, 1962); G. Johnston, "The Spirit-Paraclete in the Gospel of John," *Perspective* 9 (1968): 29–37; K. Rahner, *The Trinity* (London, G. W. H. Lampe, *God Is Spirit* (Oxford, 1977); K. McDonnell, "A

Trinitarian Theology of the Holy Spirit," *Theological Studies* 46 (1985): 191–227.

8. Paul VI, *Memoriale Domini,* May 29, 1969; see also *Immensae caritatis,* January 25, 1973.

9. Ware, "Man, Woman and the Priesthood of Christ," 9–37. Zagano, *Holy Saturday*; and others.

10. *Lumen gentium* §29; Abbott, *Vatican II,* 55–56.

11. *Lumen gentium* §28; Abbott, *Vatican II,* 53.

12. *Lumen gentium* §18–29 passim; Abbott, *Vatican II,* 37–56.

13. Hünermann, "Theologische Argumente," 119; more extensively Reininger, *Diakonat der Frau,* 606–10.

14. "Der Episkopat ist Konstructionspunkt des Amtes"; Böttigheimer, "Diakonat der Frau," 263–64; see also W. Kaspar, "Der Diakon in ecclesiologischer Sicht angesichts der gegenwärtigen Herausforderungen in Kirche und Gesellschaft," *Diaconia Christi* 32, nos. 3–4 (1997): 15–16.

15. *Lumen gentium* §29; Abbott, *Vatican II,* 55–56.

16. *Lumen gentium* §12; Abbott, *Vatican II,* 29–30.

17. **For the United States:** 63 percent of Catholics are open to women priests; Gallup Surveys on Catholics in the United States, 1987, 1993, and 1999; W. V. D'Antonio, *Laity, American and Catholic: Transforming the Church* (Kansas City, MO, 1996); M. Mason, "The Catholic Church Survey 1996," *Compass Theology Review,* December 1997, 25–31. **For Australia,** see D. McLaughlin, *The Beliefs, Values and Practices of Catholic Student Teachers* (Brisbane, 1999); etc. **National polls in Europe:** Spain 74 percent, Germany 72 percent, Portugal 71 percent, Ireland 67 percent, Italy 58 percent. At the synod in Montreal **in Canada** in 1998, 66 percent of the participants voted in favor of women as priests, 73 percent in favor of women as deacons. In **the Netherlands,** 86 percent of Catholics, including 86 percent of parish clergy and parish councils, believe that women should be admitted to priestly ordination. See T. Bernts and J. Peters, *Dichtbij en veraf: Een onderzoek in opdracht van KRO en RKK* (Hilversum, 1999), 43, 59, 153.

18. E. Hauler, *Didascaliae apostolorum fragmenta Veronensia latina* (Leipzig, 1900), pp. I–XII, and Tab. I.

19. J. Herrin, *The Formation of Christendom* (Princeton, 1987), fig. 12.

20. L. T. Lefort and J. Cochez, *Paleographisch album van gedagteekende Griekse minuskele handschiften uit de IXe en de Xe eeuw* (Louvain, 1932), p. 93.

The Texts

1. Though I would hardly claim to be a Greek scholar, my studies have given me a fair familiarity with the language. My pre-university education in the Netherlands included a high standard of Greek. Final exams required three sessions: Euripides (written), Herodotus (written), and Homer (oral). All the texts submitted were texts we had not seen previously, which we had to translate without the help of dictionaries or grammars. I took further Greek courses at the Gregorian University and the Pontifical Biblical Institute, both in Rome.

2. E. A. Nida and C. R. Taber, *The Theory and Practice of Translation* (Leiden, 1969).

3. G. Lohfink, "Weibliche Diakone im Neuen Testament," in *Die Frau im Urchristentum,* ed. G. Dautzenberg et al. (Freiburg, 1983), 320–38.

4. J. Roloff, *Der Erste Brief an Timotheus* (Neukirchen, 1988), 164; H. Merkel, *Die Pastoralbriefe* (Göttingen, 1991), 31; L. Oberlinner, *Die Pastoralbriefe* (Freiburg, 1994), 139–42.

5. H. Clark Kee, *The Origins of Christianity* (London, 1973), 51–52.

6. Commentary on 1 Corinthians 9:5, *Stromate* 3, 6, 53:3–4 GCS 52, 220, 2–25.

7. Origen, Commentary on Romans 10:17; Migne, *Patrologia graeca,* vol. 14, col. 1278 A–C. The text has been preserved in Latin, but Gryson (*Ministry of Women,* 31, 134) shows that the phrase "women deacons" must have been in Greek: "γυναικες διακονους."

8. J. W. Bickell, *Geschichte des Kirchenrechts* (Giessen, 1843), 1:127.

9. R. Gryson, *Le ministère des femmes dans l'Église ancienne* (Gembloux, 1972), 82–85. T. Schermann, *Die allgemeine Kirchenordnung des 2. Jahrhunderts* (Paderborn, 1914).

10. The meaning could be that women [the weak] are saved by men [the strong], but there may also be a reference to the well-known legend according to which the apostles, whom Christ had called "weak" (Matthew 26:41), were saved by Mary of Magdala after the resurrection. For while the apostles had lost heart, Mary stood up among them and reminded them of the Lord's teachings. See, e.g., the second-century Gospel of Mary; trans. K. L. King et al., *The Nag Hammadi Library* (San Francisco, 1988), 526–27. Such ancient texts manifest tensions that existed between men and women in ministries; K. J. Torreson, *When Women Were Priests* (San Francisco, 1995), 34–43.

11. If there was a local custom for women to sit on the floor in church ᵇe men prayed standing, this might well have been justified with a

reference to the story of Mary and Martha. Mary "sat at Jesus' feet" and this was "not to be taken from her" (Luke 10:38–42).

12. In the Latin, which is the only version available for this text, the term *diaconissa* appears, but Roger Gryson has shown, from comparisons with parallel passages in the *Apostolic Constitutions,* that the original Greek had the female ἡ διακονος, γυνη διακονος; *Ministry of Women,* 138, note 61.

13. *Didascalia* chaps. 9 and 16 (paragraph numbering by me). My translation modernizes G. Homer's in *The Didascalia Apostolorum: The Syriac Version Translated* (Oxford, 1929). Latin version in E. Tidner, *Didascaliae Apostolorum, Canonum ecclesiasticorum, Traditionis apostolicae versiones latinae* (Berlin, 1963). See also R. H. Connolly, *Didascalia Apostolorum, the Syriac Version translated and accompanied by the Verona Latin Fragments* (Oxford, 1929).

14. Read the discussion in A. C. Lochmann, *Studien zum Diakonat der Frau* (Siegen, 1996), 131–32; Ansorge, "Die wesentlichen Argumente," 582; Aubert, *Femmes diacres,* 107; Böttigheimer, "Diakonat der Frau," 258; Thiermeyer, "Diakonat der Frau," 231.

15. Mansi, *Sacrorum conciliorum,* 676–77.

16. *Panarion* 75, 1–4; Migne, *Patrologia graeca,* vol. 42, cols. 744–45; GCS 37 (1933), 478.

17. *Summary of Faith* 21; Migne, *Patrologia graeca,* vol. 42, cols. 824–25; GCS 37 (1933), 522.

18. Preserved to us only in a Latin translation by St. Jerome (Letter 51); J. Hilberg, *Corpus scriptorum ecclesiasticorum latinorum* (Vienna, 1910), 54:398.

19. As referring to ordination: A. Kalsbach, *Die altkirchliche Einrichtung der Diakonissen bis zu ihrem Erlöschen* (Freiburg, 1926), 109, note 1; as referring to consecration to continence: Gryson, *Ministry of Women,* 51–52.

20. *Letter to Amphilochius on the Canons,* Lett. 199, can. 44; R. I. Deffarari, ed., *Saint Basil: The Letters* (London, 1930), 3:130.

21. Homily 11, 1 *on the First Letter to Timothy ch. 3*; Migne, *Patrologia graeca,* vol. 62, col. 553.

22. *On the Life on St. Macrina*; Migne, *Patrologia latina,* vol. 46, cols. 988–90; English translation by W. K. Lowther Clarke, *The Life of St. Macrina* (London, 1916); P. Wilson-Kastner, "Macrina: Virgin and Teacher," *Andrews University Seminary Studies* 17 (1979): 105–17.

23. J. Mayer, *Monumenta de viduis diaconissis virginibusque tractantia* (Bonn, 1937), 18–26.

24. *Apostolic Constitutions* VIII, 28, 5; F. X. Funk, *Didascalia et constitutiones apostolorum* (Paderborn, 1905), 1:530.

25. Ansorge, "Diakonat der Frau," 46–47; Aubert, *Femmes diacres,* 105; Böttigheimer, "Diakonat der Frau," 259; Congar, *Gutachten zum Diakonat,* 37; Frohnhofen, "Weibliche Diakone," 276; Gryson, *Ministry,* 117–18; Hofrichter, *Diakonat und Frauen,* 152–54; Hünermann, *Theologische Argumente,* 104; Jensen, *Das Amt,* 59; Reininger, *Diakonat der Frau,* 97–98; Thiermeyer, "Diakonat der Frau," 230–31; Vagaggini, "L'Ordinazione delle diaconesse," 169–73.

26. Mayer, *Monumenta,* 16.

27. Migne, *Patrologia latina,* vol. 30, col. 880.

28. Migne, *Patrologia latina,* vol. 30, col. 714.

29. Migne, *Patrologia latina,* vol. 30, col. 883.

30. Although the text was originally in Greek, we only have a Latin translation of it. In *Epistolas b. Pauli Commentarii,* ed. H. B. Swete (Cambridge, 1882), 2:128–29.

31. *Epistolas,* 132–34.

32. *Epistolas,* 158–60.

33. Sozomenos, *Historia ecclesiastica,* ed. R. Hussey (Oxford, 1860), 2:812.

34. Sozomenos, *Historia Ecclesiastica,* 859.

35. *Letter to the Inhabitants of Antioch* 12:2–3; *Patres apostolici,* ed. Fr. Diekamp (Tübingen, 1913), 2:222.

36. *Interp. Epist. I ad Tim.* 3:11; Migne, *Patrologia graeca,* vol. 82, col. 809.

37. Mansi, *Sacrorum conciliorum,* 364.

38. "Lors de l'administration du baptême, les femmes ne doivent pas servir en qualité de diaconesses"; C. J. van Hefele and H. Leclercq, *Histoire des conciles,* vol. 2, 2 (Paris, 1908), 1078.

39. Severus of Antioch, *A Collection of Letters,* ed. E. W. Brooks (Paris, 1920), 245–88, 443–44; E. W. Brooks, *The Sixth Book of the Selected Letters of Severus* (London, 1903), 2:364–71.

40. Letter 49; Brooks, *Sixth Book,* 2:139.

41. Letter 62; Brooks, *Sixth Book,* 2:193–94.

42. I. Rahmani, "Chapitres qui furent écrits de l'Orient, leurs questions furent presentées aux saints Pères et elles reçurent les réponses suivantes," *Studia Syriaca* 3 (1908): 33.

43. Rahmani, "Chapitres"; see also about the text in Bar Hebraeus 7,7: A. Vööbus, *Syrische Cononessammlungen, Corpus scriptorum christianorum orientalium,* 319:499–552.

44. R. Schoell and G. Kroll, eds., *Corpus iuris civilis,* vol. 3, Novellae (Berlin, 1899), 43–45. The division in paragraphs is my own.

45. Schoell and Kroll, eds., *Corpus iuris civilis*, 3:662.

46. Schoell and Kroll, eds., *Corpus iuris civilis*, 3:616.

47. See p. 91 for a discussion of this text.

48. Jean Moschus, *Pratum spirituale* 3; Migne, *Patrologia graeca*, vol. 87, col. 2853 C.

49. Mansi, *Sacrorum conciliorum*, 949.

50. Mansi, *Sacrorum conciliorum*, 966; Mayer, *Monumenta*, 40–41.

51. Read the explanation in chapter 3, p. 19ff.

52. As in all this section, translation from the Greek is my own.

53. Vatican Library, ms. Barberini gr. 336, ff. 169r–171v; S. Parenti and E. Velkovska, *L'Eucologio Barberini gr. 336* (Rome, 2000), 170–74 and 336–39; for a description see above p. 20.

54. Sinai gr. 956; Dmitrievskij, *Opisanie*, 16.

55. Grottaferrata Γβ 1; Arranz, *L'Eucologio Constantinopolitano*, 153–60. Read the description of the ordination rite within its liturgical setting in chapter 5 above, pp. 42ff.

56. Coislinus gr. 213; Devreesse, *Le fonds Coislin*, 194–95.

57. Oxford, Bodleian auct. E.5.13; M. Arranz, *Le Typicon du Saint-Sauveur à Messine* (Rome, 1969); A. Jacob, "Un euchologe du Saint-Sauveur 'in lingua Phari' de Messine, le Bodleianus auct. E.5.13," *Bulletin de l'Institut historique belge* (1980): 283–364.

58. Morin, *Commentarius*, 78–81; see also P. Canart, *Bibliothecae Apostolicae Vaticanae codices manu scripti recensiti* (Vatican City, 1970), 423.

59. Library of the Patriarchate of Alexandria ms. 104; Dmitrievskij, *Opisanie*, 2:346–47.

60. St. Xenophon monastery gr. 163; Dmitrievskij, *Opisanie*, 2:361.

Glossary

The page references at the end of each entry indicate where a term is explained more fully.

Anachronism: placing an event, object, or person in the wrong era of time (page 50).

Anaphora: the main Byzantine eucharistic and offertory prayer (page 34).

Byzantine: belonging to the culture of the empire of Byzantium (330–1453).

Character (of a sacrament): the lasting "seal" on a person, received through baptism, confirmation, or ordination (page 54).

Cheirothesia: ordination through the laying-on of hands; from about the eighth century reserved to the installation of readers, subdeacons, and other minor orders (page 99).

Cheirotonia: ordination through the laying-on of hands; from about the eighth century this term is reserved for ordination to the priesthood, diaconate, or episcopacy (page 99).

Codex: book made up of leaves of parchment sewn together on one side, much like our books today (page 19).

Deacon: meaning "servant" in the original Greek. The term was used for both the male and the female gender, distinguished by the masculine or feminine article. In Christian communities it indicated a special ministry to which persons were assigned by ordination (page 11).

Ekphonese: second ordination prayer, softly spoken by the bishop, occurs only during the ordination to one of the three major holy orders: episcopacy, priesthood, or diaconate (page 106).

Epiclesis: the calling down of the Holy Spirit, which is the central action in any sacrament according to Eastern theology (page 104).

Euchologion: book containing the liturgy, rites, and prayers for worship in the Byzantine Christian tradition (page 20).

Folium: a leaf of parchment, abbreviated as f., with fr. standing for folium rectum (front of the page) and fv. for folium versum (back of the page) (page 21).

Form (of a sacrament): the words spoken by a minister that accompany and specify the sacred sign of a sacrament, e.g., "I absolve you from your sins" during confession (page 56).

Hegumene: meaning "governess" in Greek, used to indicate the superior of a convent of religious sisters (page 60).

Hermeneutics: the discipline of correctly interpreting a text (page 109).

Iconostasis: the sacred screen in Byzantine churches that divides, and hides, the sanctuary from the body of the church. On its front it carries images, or icons, of Christ, Mary, and the apostles (page 32).

Majuscule script: the writing of ancient Greek texts in capitals (page 23).

Manuscript: a document written by hand (page 145).

Maphorion: a large veil, draped over the head and down the shoulders, originating from Syria, that came to indicate women dedicated to God: virgins, widows, and women deacons (page 88).

Matter (of a sacrament): the physical part of the symbolism expressing a sacrament. It is further subdivided into the remote matter, e.g., the oil, and the proximate matter, e.g., the action of anointing (page 56).

Minuscule script: the use of lowercase letters in Greek manuscripts (page 23).

Myth bonding: the phenomenon that people find it hard to give up belief in an untrue story that has taken their fancy (page 117).

Neophyte: literally "new growth," used of newly baptized catechumens (page 74).

Orarion: the stole, a strip of cloth hanging down from the shoulders, that was the distinctive vestment for a deacon (page 89).

Ordination: a Roman term indicating the act of officially installing a person into a role of authority. Though Greek Christian writers at times use similar expressions when talking about the ministries, they preferred words that expressed the laying-on of hands (see cheirotonia).

Parchment: sheets of fine leather, made from lamb or goat skin specially treated to create a material for durable writing (page 19).

Rhipidion: a "fan," originally used to keep flies from food, acquired some liturgical significance in ancient Byzantine worship (page 60).

Sacrament: an external sign used in Christianity to bring about integration into sacred, interior realities. The Catholic Church recognizes only seven full sacraments: baptism, confirmation, marriage, the eucharist, penance, ordination, and the anointing of the sick (page 52).

Sacramental: ambiguous word in English. If used as an adjective, it denotes "belonging to a sacrament." If used as a noun, "a sacramental," it denotes a liturgical action that is only a blessing or dedication (page 57).

Typicon: the model from which ancient secretaries copied texts (page 27).

Validity (of a sacrament): the quality that determines whether the administering of a sacrament achieved its effect. If a baptism is declared invalid, it means it was no real baptism (page 55).

Viaticum: taking holy communion to the sick or dying (page 78).

Select bibliography

Ansorge, D. "Der Diakonat der Frau: Zum gegenwärtigen Forschungs-stand." In *Liturgie und Frauenfrage*, ed. T. Berger and A. Gerhards. St. Odilien, 1990, 31–65.

Ansorge, D. "Die wesentlichen Argumente liegen auf dem Tisch: Zur neueren Diskussion um den Diakonat der Frau." *Herder Korrespondenz* 47, no. 11 (1993): 581–86.

Aubert, M.-J. *Des femmes diacres: Un nouveau chemin pour l'Église.* Paris, 1987.

Böttigheimer, C. "Der Diakonat der Frau." *Münchener Theologische Zeitschrift* 47, no. 3 (1996): 253–66.

Bradshaw, P. F. *Ordination Rites of the Ancient Churches of East and West.* New York, 1990.

Canon Law Society of America. *The Canonical Implications of Ordaining Women to the Permanent Diaconate.* Washington, DC, 1995.

Collins, J. N. *Diakonia: Reinterpreting the Ancient Sources.* New York, 1990.

Congar, Y. "Variétés des ministères et renouveau diaconal." *Diacres aujourd'hui* (1969): 2–3.

Congar, Y. "Gutachten zum Diakonat der Frau." Amtliche Mitteilungen der Gemeinsamen Synode der Bistümer der Bundesrepublik Deutschlands, no. 7, Munich, 1973, 37–41.

Daniélou, J. *The Ministry of Women in the Early Church.* Leighton Buzzard, U.K., 1974 (originally in *Maison Dieu* 1960, no. 61).

Ditewig, W. T. "The Sacramental Identity of the Deacon." *Deacon Digest* 17, no. 1 (January/February 2000): 27–31.

FitzGerald, K. K. "The Characteristics and the Nature of the Order of the Deaconess." In *Women and the Priesthood*, ed. T. Hopko. New York, 1983, 75–95.

FitzGerald, K. K. *Women Deacons in the Orthodox Church.* Brookline, MA, 1998.

Frohnhofen, H. "Weibliche Diakone in der frühen Kirche." *Studien der Zeit* 204 (1986): 269–78.

215

Gryson, R. *The Ministry of Women in the Early Church.* Collegeville, MN, 1976; originally *Le ministère des femmes dans l'Église ancienne.* Gembloux, 1972.

Gryson, R. "Un diaconat féminin pour aujourd'hui?" *La Libre Belgique* 11.5.1981, 12 in ADCV (= *Archiv des Deutschen Caritasverbands,* Freiburg i. Breisgau). Full coding: ADCV 059.065 DdF, Fasz. 8.

Gvosdev, M. E. *The Female Diaconate: An Historical Perspective.* Minneapolis, 1991.

Hauke, M. "Überlegungen zum Weihediakonat der Frau." *Theologie und Glaube* 77 (1987): 108–27.

Hauke, M. *Women in the Priesthood.* San Francisco, 1988.

Hauke, M. "Diakonat der Frau?" *Forum für Kirche und Theologie* 12, no. 1 (1996): 36–45.

Hauke, M. "Der Frauendiakonat als Hebel zur Veränderung der Kirche." *Forum für Kirche und Theologie* 14, no. 2 (1998): 132–47.

Hilberath, B. J. "Das Amt der Diakonin: Ein sakramentales Amt?" In *Diakonat: Ein Amt für Frauen in der Kirche — Ein frauengerechtes Amt?* Ostfildern, 1997, 212–18.

Hofrichter, P. "Diakonat und Frauen im kirchlichen Amt." *Heiliger Dienst* 50, no. 3 (1996): 140–58.

Hoping, H. "Diakonat der Frau ohne Frauenpriestertum?" *Schweizerische Kirchenzeitung* 18 (June 14, 2000).

Hopko, T., ed. *Women and the Priesthood.* New York, 1983.

Hünermann, P. "Gutachten zur Bestellung des Diakons (der Diakonin) zum ordentlichen Spender der Krankensalbung." *Diaconia Christi* 9, no. 3 (1974): 25–28.

Hünermann, P. "Conclusions Regarding the Female Diaconate." *Theological Studies* 36 (1975): 325–33.

Hünermann, P. "Stellungnahme zu den Anmerkungen von Professor Otto Semmelroth SJ betreffend Votum der Synode zum Weihediakonat der Frau." *Diaconia Christi* 10, no. 1 (1975): 33–38.

Hünermann, P. "Diakonat — ein Beitrag zur Erneuerung des kirchlichen Amtes? Wider-Holung." *Diakonia Christi* 29 (1994): 13–22.

Hünermann, P. "Lehramtliche Dokumente zur Frauenordination." In *Frauenordination,* ed. Walter Groß. Munich, 1996, 83–96.

Hünermann, P. "Theologische Argumente für die Diakonatsweihe von Frauen." In *Diakonat: Ein Amt für Frauen in der Kirche — Ein frauengerechtes Amt?* Ostfildern, 1997, 98–128.

Jensen, A. *Gottes selbstbewußte Töchter: Frauenemanzipation im frühen Christentum?* Freiburg, 1992.

Jensen, A. "Das Amt der Diakonin in der kirchlichen Tradition der ersten Jahrtausend." In *Diakonat: Ein Amt für Frauen in der Kirche — Ein frauengerechtes Amt?* Ostfildern, 1997, 33–52.

Jorissen, H. "Theologische Bedenken gegen die Diakonatsweihe von Frauen." In *Diakonat: Ein Amt für Frauen in der Kirche — Ein frauengerechtes Amt?* Ostfildern, 1997, 86–97.

Kalsbach, A. *Die altkirchliche Einrichtung der Diakonissen bis zu ihrem Erlöschen.* Freiburg, 1926.

Kalsbach, A. "Diakonisse." *Reallexikon für Antike und Christentum.* Stuttgart, 1957, vol. 3, cols. 917–28.

Kaspar, W. "Der Diakon in ecclesiologischer Sicht angesichts der gegenwärtigen Herausforderungen in Kirche und Gesellschaft." *Diaconia Christi* 32, nos. 3–4 (1997): 13–33; English: "The Ministry of the Deacon." *Deacon Digest* 15, no. 2 (March–April 1998), 19–27.

Lochmann, A. C. *Studien zum Diakonat der Frau.* Siegen, 1996.

Lohfink, G. "Weibliche Diakone im Neuen Testament." In *Die Frau im Urchristentum,* ed. G. Dautzenberg et al. Freiburg, 1983, 320–38.

Luislampe, P. "Diakonat der Frau." In *Diakonat der Frau — Chance für die Zukunft?* Münster, 1996, 23–36.

Martimort, A.-G. "La question du service des femmes à l'autel." *Notitiae* 16 (1980): 8–16.

Martimort, A.-G. *Les diaconesses: Essai historique* (Eph. Lit. Subs. 24), Rome, 1982; English translation by K. D. Whitehead: *Deaconesses: An Historical Study.* San Francisco, 1986.

McManus, F. R. "Book Review: Diaconesses: An Historical Study." *The Jurist* 47 (1987): 596–98.

Merklein, H., and K. Müller, eds. *Die Frau im Urchristentum.* Freiburg, 1983.

Müller, G. *Priestertum und Diakonat.* Einsiedeln, 2000; English translation: *Priesthood and Diaconate.* San Francisco, 2002.

Rahner, K., and H. Vorgrimler, eds. *Diaconia in Christo.* Quaestiones Disputatae 15. Freiburg, 1962.

Raming, I. "Bestrebungen zum Diakonat der Frau im 20. Jahrhundert." In *Diakonat der Frau — Chance für die Zukunft? Dokumentation zu den Tagungen am 18. Mai 1993 and 19. Mai 1995 in der Katholisch-Sozialen Akademie,* ed. A. Urban. Münster, 1995.

Reininger, D. *Diakonat der Frau in der einen Kirche.* Ostfildern, 1999.

Sattler, D. "Zur Sacramentalität des Diakonats der Frau." In *Diakonat: Ein Amt für Frauen in der Kirche — Ein frauengerechtes Amt?* Ostfildern, 1997, 219–24.

Schottroff, L. *Lydias ungeduldige Schwestern: Feministische Sozialgeschichte des frühen Christentums*. Gütersloh, 1994.

Semmelroth, O. "Anmerkungen zu dem Votum der Synode zum Weihediakonat der Frau." *Diaconia Christi* 10, no. 1 (1975): 29–32.

Swidler, A., and V. Ratigan. *A New Phoebe: Perspectives on Roman Catholic Women and the Permanent Diaconate*. Kansas City, MO, 1990.

Synek, E. M. *Heilige Frauen der frühen Christenheit: Zu den Frauen-bildern in hagiograpischen Texten des christlichen Ostens* (= Das östliche Christentum, NF 48). Würzburg, 1994.

Theodorou, E. *The "Ordination"* [χειροτονια] *or "Appointment"* (χειρο-θεσια) *of Women Deacons*. Athens, 1954.

Theodorou, E. "The Ministry of Women in the Greek Orthodox Church." In *Orthodox Women: Their Role and Participation in the Orthodox Church*, ed. World Council of Churches (Geneva, 1977), 37–43.

Theodorou, E. "Das Amt der Diakoninnen in der kirchlichen Tradition: Ein orthodoxer Beitrag zum Problem der Frauenordination." *Una Sancta* 33 (1978): 162–72.

Theodorou, E. "The Institution of Deaconesses in the Orthodox Church and the Possibility of its Restoration." In *The Place of the Woman in the Orthodox Church and the Question of the Ordination of Women*, ed. G. Limouris (Katerini, Greece, 1992), 207–38.

Thiermeyer, A. "Der Diakonat der Frau." *Theologisch Quartalschrift* 173, no. 3 (1993): 226–36; also in *Frauenordination*, ed. W. Gross. Munich, 1966, 53–63.

Vagaggini, C. "L'Ordinazione delle diaconesse nella tradizione greca e bizantina." *Orientalia Christiana Periodica* 40 (1974): 145–89.

Vorgrimler, H. "Gutachten über die Diakonatsweihe für Frauen." *Diaconia Christi* 9, no. 3 (1974): 19–24.

Ware, K. "Man, Woman and the Priesthood of Christ." In *Women and the Priesthood*, ed. T. Hopko. New York, 1983, 9–37.

Wijngaards, John. *The Ordination of Women in the Catholic Church: Unmasking a Cuckoo's Egg Tradition*. London and New York, 2001.

Zagano, P. *Holy Saturday: An Argument for the Restoration of the Female Diaconate in the Catholic Church*. New York, 2000.

Index

Of Related Interest

Anthony P. Kowalski
MARRIED CATHOLIC PRIESTS
Their History, Their Journeys, TMinusculeheir Reflections

Is ordaining married men the solution to the shortage of celibate male Catholic priests? *Married Catholic Priests* shows the remarkable experience of American Catholic priests who marry. In part a fascinating historical review, the book includes varied experiences of married priests in our time, whether active in the church or not. Kowalski manifests a strong faith, a positive affirmation of church and priesthood, and a welcoming embrace of the stirrings of the Spirit in these times.

"Wonderfully instructive about married popes, bishops, and priests of the first millennium, Kowalski traces the moves toward a celibate clergy in the West before he turns to the pre- and post-conciliar period. Perhaps the most interesting part reports the shame and humiliation visited on married priests and their wives balanced by accounts of those who have continued active in church life, some on the national scene. The book makes one ask how and when the Roman See will set up vicariates like those of Opus Dei and the military chaplaincies to reinstate the active service in any diocese those who wish to resume priestly ministry."

—Gerard S. Sloyan, author of *Preaching from the Lectionary*

0-8245-2349-0, $19.95, paperback

crossroad

Of Related Interest

Phyllis Zagano
HOLY SATURDAY
An Argument for
the Restoration of the Female Diaconate
in the Catholic Church

A serious effort to faithfully investigate the history and canonical viability of the female diaconate. Based on thorough research, as well as sound historical and theological analysis and reflection, this book makes a significant contribution to the discussion and development of women's roles in the modern church.

Holy Saturday has succeeded in both enriching and helping to shape the discussion regarding the restoration of women to the diaconate in the Catholic Church. It has inspired reading and discussion groups, countless Internet chats, and serious discussion and scholarly reviews in both academic and ecclesiastical circles.

0-8245-1832-2, $16.95, paperback

Check your local bookstore for availability.
To order directly from the publisher,
please call 1-800-707-0670 for Customer Service
or visit our website at *www.cpcbooks.com.*
For catalog orders, please send your request to the address below.

THE CROSSROAD PUBLISHING COMPANY
16 Penn Plaza, Suite 1550
New York, NY 10001

All prices subject to change.

crossroad